YORK NOTES

Mansfield Park

Jane Austen

Note by Delia Dick

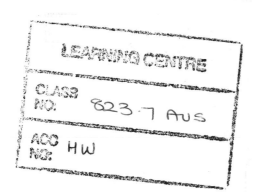

Longman   York Press

YORK PRESS
322 Old Brompton Road, London SW5 9JH

PEARSON EDUCATION LIMITED
Edinburgh Gate, Harlow,
Essex CM20 2JE, United Kingdom
Associated companies, branches and representatives throughout the world

First published 1999
Second impression 2000

ISBN 0-582-41457-1

Designed by Vicki Pacey
Phototypeset by Gem Graphics, Trenance, Mawgan Porth, Cornwall
Colour reproduction and film output by Spectrum Colour
Produced by Pearson Education China Limited, Hong Kong

C ONTENTS

032078

PART ONE

INTRODUCTION

HOW TO STUDY A NOVEL

Studying a novel on your own requires self-discipline and a carefully thought-out work plan in order to be effective.

- You will need to read the novel more than once. Start by reading it quickly for pleasure, then read it slowly and thoroughly.
- On your second reading make detailed notes on the plot, characters and themes of the novel. Further readings will generate new ideas and help you to memorise the details of the story.
- Some of the characters will develop as the plot unfolds. How do your responses towards them change during the course of the novel?
- Think about how the novel is narrated. From whose point of view are events described?
- A novel may or may not present events chronologically: the time-scheme may be a key to its structure and organisation.
- What part do the settings play in the novel?
- Are words, images or incidents repeated so as to give the work a pattern? Do such patterns help you to understand the novel's themes?
- Identify what styles of language are used in the novel.
- What is the effect of the novel's ending? Is the action completed and closed, or left incomplete and open?
- Does the novel present a moral and just world?
- Cite exact sources for all quotations, whether from the text itself or from critical commentaries. Wherever possible find your own examples from the novel to back up your opinions.
- Always express your ideas in your own words.

This York Note offers an introduction to *Mansfield Park* and cannot substitute for close reading of the text and the study of secondary sources.

The wit and elegance of Jane Austen's style have been admired ever since her novels first appeared. But there is emotional turbulence, too, beneath the urbane surface of her prose: heroines hope and suffer for love, the devious betray, friends are at cross purposes, the snobbish patronise and the humble often triumph.

Mansfield Park has a heroine from a long tradition of storytelling: Fanny Price is the poor relation charitably adopted into the family of her wealthy uncle, Sir Thomas Bertram – she is permitted to enjoy some of the advantages this can offer her but not, of course, to aspire to the same social standing as her cousins. One aunt is cruel to her; the rest of the family are indifferent rather than unkind. Only her cousin Edmund, with whom she is soon in love, understands and cares for her. Something of a Cinderella figure, Fanny – virtuous, and timid at first – is able finally to win the heroine's anticipated happy ending.

A consistent vein of comedy runs through the novel, to be observed not least in the memorable set pieces: the visit by the group of young people to Sotherton, where the lovers and would-be lovers are all at cross purposes; the first – and last – rehearsal of the improper *Lovers' Vows*; the confusion of Fanny's return to her original home in Portsmouth.

Yet Jane Austen is no gentle observer of the mores of that segment of society with which she deals. Her **irony** bites deep, not least in her comments about the relationship between marriage and money. *Mansfield Park* is probably the darkest of her novels, full of ambivalence and contradictions about the status of the property and its inhabitants. 'Home' is established for Fanny as Mansfield Park, the source of all contentment as far as she is concerned. Her visit, after many years, to her original home in Portsmouth results in disillusion: she finds only noise and disorder and the expected emotional reunion does not materialise. She no longer belongs there. So Mansfield Park is established as superior in every way to Portsmouth; yet it is from the insalubrious house at Portsmouth that the sterling characters of Fanny and her sailor brother, William, emerge. Of the four Bertram offspring of Mansfield Park, three turn out to be unprincipled and wilful, at the very least – Sir Thomas's heir is a dissipated spendthrift, his elder daughter's adultery makes her unacceptable in polite society and his younger daughter barely escapes the same fate.

Nevertheless, it is not necessarily the virtuous characters of the novel who attract the reader. The escape from constraints symbolised by the wanderings at Sotherton, and the romantic opportunities offered by the amateur dramatics are likely to be viewed with some sympathy. The worldly Crawfords are on the one hand seen as a corrupt influence, bringing a kind of infection from sophisticated London; on the other hand the reader understands their social popularity and vivacity. The usual regime at Mansfield Park seems oppressive and limiting, even in the context of the period.

The novel has its detractors as well as its admirers: in particular, its heroine, Fanny, has always aroused extreme views. *Mansfield Park* offers the reader an opportunity to make some difficult judgements about Jane Austen's purpose.

S<small>UMMARIES & COMMENTARIES</small>

T<small>HE SELECTED TEXT</small>

The text referred to in this Note is the 1996 Penguin Classics edition, edited by Kathryn Sutherland.

There have been many editions of *Mansfield Park* since the first, published by Thomas Egerton in 1814. This cost eighteen shillings for the three volumes in board covers – expensive at the time. Jane Austen was not altogether satisfied with Egerton's integrity: he published a second edition of the popular *Pride and Prejudice* without her knowledge. The second edition of *Mansfield Park*, a year before Jane Austen's death, was published by John Murray in 1816. That edition, with some editorial and other alterations, is the form on which most subsequent publications have been based.

However, as the editor of the selected text points out, there are advantages in going back to the first edition, which she believes has a freshness that tends to be lost in revision. Kathryn Sutherland has therefore edited the 1814 version, giving subsequent variations at the end of the work.

The modern reader will find punctuation that does not accord with current practice, as well as one or two colloquial grammatical usages and some erratic spellings, which are probably Jane Austen's own. Egerton's original editing, if any, is certainly not heavy-handed: capitalisation of nouns, for instance, is inconsistent; and no editorial eye seems to have spotted that Lady Bertram's favourite dog, Pug, apparently changes sex during the year or so of the main action.

E<small>DITIONS AFTER</small> 1816

Following the editions of 1814 and 1816 (and all based entirely upon, or taking as authoritative, the latter), key publications are, briefly:

1816: The first complete translation into French (*Le Parc de Mansfield, ou Les Trois Cousines*)

1832: The first American edition

1833 (reprinted 1866, 1869, 1878–9, 1882): Cheap, one-volume, illustrated version in Bentley's Standard Novels series (which included the rest of Austen's published work)

1892: A ten-volume edition of Austen's novels, reprinted the same year, published by J.M. Dent and revised in 1966 as the Everyman editions

1923: R.W. Chapman's scholarly edition of the novels for the Clarendon Press, which has remained the standard authority, still with the emphasis on an 1816 reading

At the end of the twentieth century, many editions of Jane Austen's work are available, including inexpensive paperbacks and taped versions. The modern reader also often has the opportunity to evaluate the dramatisations of her work in films and television series. In even the most successful of these some of the delights of the text are bound to be lost. Nevertheless, these visualisations often very carefully suggest the settings and dress of which her first readers needed no description but which can be helpful at something approaching two hundred years later.

SYNOPSIS

Thirty years before the main events of the novel are recounted, the three Misses Ward married very differently. The best-looking sister, Maria, made an unexpectedly successful society marriage with Sir Thomas Bertram of Mansfield Park. He is a prosperous and principled man who sits in Parliament and has business interests beyond his Northampton estates, in Antigua. They have two sons and two daughters. Maria's elder sister married a clergyman, the Rev. Mr Norris. They live in the nearby Parsonage and their marriage is childless. Mrs Norris is left a widow soon after the main story begins. The youngest sister, Frances, wilfully married a Lieutenant Price of the Marines. With her large family she lives at

Portsmouth in something approaching poverty, alienated from her sisters.

As a move towards reconciliation, the self-important Mrs Norris proposes that she and the Bertrams should help the unfortunate Mrs Price, about to give birth to her ninth infant, by offering a home to her eldest daughter; the story proper begins as Fanny Price, the novel's central character, arrives at Mansfield Park at the age of ten. She is small, shy and not very robust, unlike her cousins, who are all older than Fanny. Maria and Julia Bertram are well grown, confident and well educated (to their own satisfaction at least); they tease her. Sir Thomas's intentions are kindly, but he appears stern. Lady Bertram, lazy and selfish, is kindly too but little interested in the child. Aunt Norris, who has decided that the burden of Fanny's upbringing should fall entirely upon the Bertrams, is a snobbish and spiteful woman, who treats Fanny with real malice. Fanny's cousin Tom, the heir to Mansfield Park, is careless and extravagant; the younger brother, Edmund, who is destined for the clergy, saves her from despair by noticing her homesickness and generally wretched state. He shows a genuine interest in her qualities; their friendship as the years pass becomes important to both and inevitably Fanny falls in love with him.

When Fanny is eighteen, Sir Thomas, taking Tom with him, goes to attend to business affairs in Antigua. In his absence, the meddling Mrs Norris promotes an engagement between Maria and a wealthy but feeble-witted young landowner, Mr Rushworth of Sotherton. The somewhat staid existence at Mansfield is greatly enlivened by the arrival of the dashing Crawfords, who are visiting their half-sister, Mrs Grant, wife of the new parson. Mary Crawford and her brother Henry are wealthy and worldly – they quickly become very popular with the young Bertrams. Henry is soon observed to be flirting with both Julia and the informally engaged Maria. Fanny is miserable as she sees that Edmund is attracted to the charming Mary.

The younger Bertrams, the Crawfords, Mrs Norris and Fanny make an expedition to Sotherton, the grand seat of Mr Rushworth. It turns out to be a trying day for most of those involved. After viewing the great house, the party breaks up to wander through the grounds. Henry, who has flirted with Julia on the way, now manages to escape into the great park with Maria, who tricks her fiancé into returning to the house. Mary, who is recognising a reciprocal attraction to Edmund, discovers to her horror that he is to be a clergyman (her cynicism about the profession has already been revealed); nevertheless, she and Edmund abandon Fanny on a seat in the wilderness and wander off on their own. Mr Rushworth is angry and bewildered and Julia, too, is cross, although she returns to favour with Henry on the journey home. Only the unperceptive Mrs Norris is happy, seeing the visit as a personal triumph.

Tom returns to England ahead of his father and arrives at Mansfield Park with one of his many friends, the Hon. John Yates. It is Yates who introduces the idea of family theatricals. Both Edmund and Fanny are dismayed, not least because they know that the absent Sir Thomas would never countenance such an unseemly enterprise. However, Tom and Yates carry the day, Lady Bertram little interested, as usual, and Mrs Norris seeing an opportunity for exercising her imagined organising skills. The preparations for the performance of *Lovers' Vows* compound the pattern of love interests established on the visit to Sotherton. With rehearsals offering opportunities for romantic developments, Henry's flirtation with Maria becomes more obvious; the deceived Mr Rushworth has to be placated, while Julia sulks. Edmund is eventually drawn in, against his will, and poor Fanny is obliged to help Mary Crawford rehearse a love scene with him.

The scheme takes on ever more elaborate dimensions, with a built stage and sets disturbing the well-planned furnishings of Sir Thomas's rooms, and invitations to the play issued widely by Tom. The first full rehearsal has begun to take place, with even Fanny having to take a minor role, when a sudden commotion announces the unexpectedly early return of Sir Thomas. He is pleased to see his family again, and notices Fanny's improved looks particularly favourably. With little fuss, he puts an end to the amateur dramatics and sets the house to rights. He is disappointed that Edmund had not known better what was fitting, and his confidence in Mrs Norris diminishes sharply from this point.

Henry Crawford leaves the Parsonage without making the proposal Maria had hoped for. Her father soon realises Mr Rushworth's inadequacies and presses Maria as to her real feelings for him. She is not prepared to give up the position in society he offers and they are married. Julia goes with the couple to Brighton. Sir Thomas's approval of Fanny grows and, as the only young woman in the house, she gains status and more confidence. Her uncle invites her brother William (who he has befriended and who is on leave from the navy) to visit and she spends a happy time with him, which culminates in a ball arranged by Sir Thomas.

Meanwhile, Henry Crawford has returned and confides in his sister Mary that he intends to make Fanny fall in love with him. Mary, who is now friendly with Fanny, is not averse – after her initial surprise – to helping him in his proposed flirtation. She pleads his case and persuades Fanny to borrow a necklace to wear at the ball, which she later admits her brother has bought. This embarrasses Fanny, whose distrust of Henry has not diminished as she has observed his romantic entanglements with Maria and Julia. Fortunately, the necklace is too large to carry the amber cross that William has given her, and Edmund presents her with a more modest chain, which she is happy to wear, although politeness compels her to wear the Crawfords' gift, too. She looks well at the ball and, though still shy, is able to take her position in society as Sir Thomas's niece.

Henry Crawford makes obvious his admiration for Fanny, much to her dismay. He has in fact taken up the challenge he sees in her indifference to him and determines to marry her. He befriends William, using the influence of his uncle, the admiral, to secure William's promotion. With this news, he approaches Fanny and, relying on her gratitude on William's behalf, proposes to her. In spite of Fanny's uncompromising rejection, Henry perseveres with his courtship. Fanny suffers the grave displeasure of Sir Thomas, who cannot understand how Fanny can refuse such an excellent offer. Lady Bertram tells her it is her duty to accept and even Edmund, returning from ordination, believes she will grow to love Henry Crawford, of whom he thinks highly. Fanny's misery is extended by the knowledge that Edmund is thinking of proposing to Mary Crawford.

Sir Thomas decides that Fanny should pay a visit to her family in Portsmouth, believing that the discomfort of life there may bring her to a new appreciation of what Henry Crawford is offering her through marriage. Accompanied by William and at first excited at the prospect of going 'home', Fanny's romantic view of the reunion is soon put in perspective: her mother is a distracted and incompetent housewife with poorly controlled servants, her father's manner is coarse and her brothers and sisters noisy and disorderly. Only the older of her sisters, Susan, is congenial, and Fanny does what she can to befriend her. Finding the dirt and discomfort beyond remedy, and her presence of little interest to her family, she is soon yearning for Mansfield Park, which she now knows to be her true home. She is dependent for news upon letters from her regular correspondent, Lady Bertram, and from Mary Crawford, who continues to promote her brother's interest in Fanny. Henry unexpectedly visits her; she is impressed by his tactful behaviour and relieved that her family are seen at their best.

As Fanny's visit becomes extended beyond the two months originally planned, she is shocked by the increasing worldliness shown in Mary Crawford's correspondence, learns of the debauched Tom's serious illness and return to Mansfield Park, and hears a rumour about Henry and Maria. She finally gets confirmation that Maria has left her husband for Henry, and that Yates and Julia have eloped.

Edmund, distraught at the disgrace and at Mary Crawford's unprincipled attitude to her brother's behaviour, comes to Portsmouth to collect Fanny and her sister. In spite of the illness and shame which has overwhelmed the Bertrams, Fanny cannot help but feel happy. Edmund has given up Mary, and Fanny is badly needed at Mansfield Park; she returns to take up what is now a central position in the household.

The final chapter describes Sir Thomas's soul-searchings over his inadequacies as a father, Tom's gradual recovery and the failure of the relationship between Maria and Henry Crawford: Maria cannot now be accepted in society and, a punishment perhaps even worse, Mrs Norris goes to live with her as her companion. The runaway marriage of Julia and Yates achieves respectability, William's naval career flourishes and, finally, there is a happy ending for Fanny when her beloved Edmund comes to his senses sooner than might be expected and recognises that she is the wife for him.

VOLUME I

CHAPTER 1 (VOLUME I, CHAPTER i)

Three sisters marry

In a prologue to the main story, the reader learns of the varying fortunes in marriage, some thirty years before, of the three handsome

Ward sisters. The middle sister, Maria, in spite of her relatively modest dowry, made a move upwards in the social scale when she married Sir Thomas Bertram of Mansfield Park. Her husband, a wealthy Northamptonshire landowner, was able to assist the elder Miss Ward by finding her a clergyman husband amongst his friends and presenting the Rev. Mr Norris with a comfortable living at Mansfield Park. Frances, the youngest sister, married very imprudently – an elopement is implied. Her husband, Mr Price, an uneducated Lieutenant of Marines without useful 'connections', was considered a poor match by her family, and Mrs Price bitterly ended contact with her sisters. At the time the main narrative begins, she is expecting her ninth child and is in increasingly difficult financial circumstances in Portsmouth.

An appeal to the wealthy Bertrams does not go unheeded. They respond with practical aid and advice; it is later proposed by the childless Mrs Norris that one of the Price children should be taken in and brought up at Mansfield Park, with the duty to be shared by herself and the Bertrams. Sir Thomas, a principled and cautious man, considers the implications and finally agrees that the eldest Price daughter should be accepted into the family, with her future provided for. However, he is keen that a distance in status is maintained between Fanny and the Bertram daughters, of whom there are two, as well as two sons. To Sir Thomas's surprise, Mrs Norris is not expecting the girl to live with her, but entirely at the Bertrams'. Nevertheless, the invitation is issued and quickly accepted.

> There is much for the reader to learn from this opening chapter. The background to the main narrative is established and the characteristics of the older generation are outlined: of the three sisters, Lady Bertram is 'a woman of very tranquil feelings, and a temper remarkably easy and indolent'; Mrs Norris has an ominous 'spirit of activity' which warns of her busybody nature; Mrs Price appeals to her rich sister with much 'despondence, such a superfluity of children, and such a want of almost every thing else', giving a picture of her near poverty in Portsmouth. Sir Thomas Bertram's secure position in society is made clear. Although he can do nothing for Lieutenant Price, he is prepared to extend his patronage where he can to assist those connected with him by

family ties. He thinks ahead to what may be the consequences of adopting Mrs Price's daughter, and his charitable intention includes a socially conscious view of the elevated position of himself and his daughters in relation to the child from Portsmouth. The reader is inclined to agree with Mrs Price's earlier 'disrespectful reflections on the pride of Sir Thomas'.

The narrative **voice** of this chapter sets the tone for the novel as a whole. The narrator is detached and writes with wit and humour of the nature of marriage amongst the genteel segment of society identified. In this view, with the reader's amused agreement implied, money is closely linked with marriage, and the necessity for financial prudence in would-be brides overrides all else. Frances Ward's predicament provides an awful lesson; however, few girls could expect, 'with only seven thousand pounds' like her sister, to marry a wealthy baronet because, in the narrator's memorably ironic words, 'there certainly are not so many men of large fortune in the world, as there are pretty women to deserve them.' (See Textual Analysis for a detailed commentary on the opening to the novel.)

no interest could reach no influence or patronage could be brought to bear
the attack on Nanny's cousin the proposed imposition on Nanny's cousin, the sadler (unacceptable to Sir Thomas as a suitable lodging for even a lowly member of his family)

CHAPTER 2 (VOLUME I, CHAPTER ii)

Fanny Price arrives at Mansfield Park

Fanny Price, aged ten, meets the Bertrams. In spite of the admonitions of her Aunt Norris on the journey to Northamptonshire, she is shy and too frightened to respond to the well-meant overtures of Sir Thomas and Lady Bertram. Her uncle appears stern and her cousins, Tom and Edmund, seventeen and sixteen respectively, have 'the grandeur of men' in her eyes. Her other cousins are Maria, thirteen, and Julia, twelve; the girls are confident, good-looking and well grown for their ages – unlike the small and timid Fanny. They patronise her, the servants make fun of her clothes and the girls' governess is surprised at her lack of what the Bertrams consider to be necessary education.

The unhappy child, used to an important position as eldest daughter at Portsmouth, and particularly missing her older brother William, is wretchedly homesick, although no one notices this until Edmund finds her crying on the attic stairs. He comforts her, arranges for her to correspond with William, and generally takes her under his wing. With a real friend in the house, Fanny gradually becomes 'more comfortable'. Sir Thomas begins to feel that his benevolence has been worthwhile, and extends his assistance to the Price boys, inviting William to stay for a week at Mansfield Park before he goes to sea as a sailor. The two siblings' 'eager affection' and 'hours of happy mirth', as well as 'moments of serious conference', offer a joyful interlude for Fanny, whose Portsmouth family seem to have forgotten her.

Fanny becomes an accepted member of the family at Mansfield, although she is little noticed and it is generally agreed that she falls far short of her cousins in appearance and abilities. Only Edmund recognises the strengths of her character and her natural cleverness, trying to help her overcome her diffidence and 'giving her advice, consolation, and encouragement'.

In spite of the humorous tone, the poor relation's miseries as a homesick child amongst well-meaning but largely indifferent rich relations are quite painfully conveyed.

Education plays a central role in this chapter, with Austen having quite a bit of fun at the expense of what was considered the 'advanced' education of the day, as enjoyed by the Bertram girls. In fact, the characters of Maria and Julia are to a fair degree defined in terms of this education, of which Sir Thomas is so proud until he sees its deficiencies at the end of the narrative. His daughters' minds have been packed with snippets of information selected from history, geography, natural history and astronomy; their 'accomplishments' include watercolour painting and music. Their self-confidence – boosted by Mrs Norris's sycophantic admiration – and their education – expensive and up-to-date as it is – have left them 'entirely deficient in the less common acquirements of self-knowledge, generosity, and humility'.

regaled delighted

half a guinea a gold coin – a useful gift, worth something near to the average working man's weekly wage at the time

CHAPTER 3 (VOLUME I, CHAPTER iii)

Mrs Norris is put out; Sir Thomas leaves for Antigua

Five years pass. Sir Thomas has some financial anxieties: he is angry with his elder son and heir, Tom, who has developed an extravagant and selfish lifestyle which eats into the income of the Mansfield estate. In particular, this means that the living (the nearby Parsonage) – intended for Edmund, who is to be ordained as a clergyman – will have to be leased out, leaving for Edmund a less desirable benefice slightly further away. The Parsonage has become vacant because of the death of the Rev. Mr Norris, whose widow moves into a small house in the village.

Sir Thomas, looking for ways to reduce his expenses, believes that his sister-in-law will now welcome the opportunity to share the upbringing of Fanny, and will take her to live with her as companion. Fanny is utterly dismayed by this suggestion, as Aunt Norris has never shown anything but disdain and even malice towards her. Her anxieties are soon relieved, however, since Mrs Norris is very put out, and will hear of no such thing, pleading poverty and lack of room in her new house. She takes a dislike to the new incumbent at the Parsonage, Dr Grant, and especially to his wife, who provides a lavish table, which the mean Mrs Norris considers inappropriate to her station.

Losses at his West Indies estate cause Sir Thomas to set off a year later on the hazardous journey to Antigua, in an attempt to rectify matters. He takes Tom with him, to distract him from his expensive pleasures, and leaves Fanny with permission to invite William to stay when he next has leave. She is mortified by Sir Thomas's parting remark that she is too childish and that William might 'find his sister at sixteen in some respects too much like his sister at ten'.

Sir Thomas's character is further developed in this chapter, in particular by the views on his absence held by other members of his family. Lady Bertram, to whom the adjective 'indolent' is frequently applied, 'did not at all like to have her husband leave her' but shows no understanding of the dangers of his journey; his daughters show great relief at the removal of his oppressive presence. He had never seemed 'the friend of their pleasures' and they enjoy a sense of freedom from restraint. Fanny, too, feels relief at the departure of her stern uncle; she, however, feels remorse that she has no warmer feelings towards the man who has done so much for her family.

would soon pop off would soon die

CHAPTER 4 (VOLUME I, CHAPTER iv)

Fanny's horse, Maria's engagement and the arrival of the Crawfords

Fanny had earlier been given a pony to ride, as an aid to improving her health. When it dies, she is left without the possibility of suitable exercise; her aunts suggest that she could ride one of her cousins' horses when not in use but, when the weather is fit, the horses are always out with Maria and Julia. Edmund comes to her rescue, ensuring that there is a horse in his own stable that is suitable and always available for Fanny.

Now twenty years old, Maria Bertram is 'beginning to think matrimony a duty' and becomes engaged informally to Mr Rushworth of Sotherton. His mother and Mrs Norris, who have worked energetically to this end, are very satisfied; Maria enjoys the prospect of sharing in an income larger than her father's and – most desirably – having a house in London as well as in the country. Only Edmund is doubtful, thinking to himself frequently, 'If this man had not twelve thousand a year, he would be a very stupid fellow.'

Mansfield society is enlivened not only by the return, ahead of his father, of Tom, but also by the arrival of the wealthy, young and dashing brother and sister, Henry and Mary Crawford. They are visiting their half-sister, Mrs Grant, at the Parsonage; Mary intends to make her home there since their widowed guardian, a retired admiral, exhibits 'vicious conduct' by bringing his mistress into his London home.

Edmund's thoughtfulness and good sense are illustrated in this chapter: the first in his tactful arrangements for Fanny to have a suitable mare at her disposal, the second in his doubts about the dim-witted Mr Rushworth's suitability as a husband for Maria.

The novel opened with an **ironic** account of materialistic marriage; this theme is developed at the end of this chapter, with three views: Henry explains his promiscuous creed, with marriage to be put off for as long as possible; the more romantic Mrs Grant defends the institution of marriage, saying if anyone shows 'a disinclination for it, I only set it down that they have not yet seen the right person'; Mary approves of marriage, she claims, but her sophisticated attitude contrasts with that of her half-sister when she says 'every body should marry as soon as they can do it to advantage'.

Fanny had just reached her eighteenth year i.e. Fanny had just turned seventeen

'Heaven's *last* best gift' from John Milton's *Paradise Lost* (Book V, line 19) – Crawford jokingly sees marriage as a last resort

CHAPTER 5 (VOLUME I, CHAPTER V)

The Bertrams and the Crawfords meet; is Fanny 'out' or 'not out'?

The young people meet and find each other congenial company. Both Maria and Julia are attracted to Henry and he is prepared to exploit the opportunities for flirtation; Mary casts a materialistic eye over Tom's likely inheritance and begins to consider marrying into the Bertram family.

She is puzzled by Fanny's status in the household. The reader knows already that, when Maria and Julia go to balls and other social events, Fanny stays behind as companion to her Aunt Bertram. She is eighteen and old enough to be 'out' in society, but Mary notices that Fanny rarely speaks in company. After Tom has recounted an anecdote about an inadvertent breach of etiquette on his part, Mary decides that Fanny is, in fact, 'not out'.

The attitudes towards members of the opposite sex, already outlined in relation to the Crawfords in the previous chapter, are amplified here. Henry Crawford enjoys making women fall in love with him, which begins to seem not so much a harmless activity, but more to do with the exercise of power over those of the opposite sex. Mary's attitude to marriage is seen as quite bitter – she speaks of marriage partners being 'taken in' and says 'it is, of all transactions, the one in which people expect most from others, and are least honest themselves'. The example of the 'vicious' admiral, the Crawfords' uncle, has already been suggested as a bad example. Mrs Grant speaks up for tolerance in marriage.

Fanny's Cinderella-like status is underlined in this chapter. The reader knows, from the previous chapter, that Fanny stays at home when the sisters go out, and listens to their accounts of balls with no expectation of going herself. She has taken over one of the ex-governess's duties, as companion to Lady Bertram in the evenings. The anomaly of her situation is noticed by the socially conscious Mary Crawford; the idea that Fanny might be expected to enter into the usual social world of a young woman of the Bertram family does not seem to have occurred to anyone at Mansfield Park.

quizzing teasing

CHAPTER 6 (VOLUME I, CHAPTER vi)

Dinner at Mansfield Park; Mr Rushworth's 'improvements' and Miss Crawford's harp

Tom has gone away to the races – he has a likely runner – and Edmund takes on the role of head of the house at a dinner party: the Bertrams' guests are the Crawfords, Mr Rushworth, Mrs Norris, and Dr and Mrs Grant. The main subject of discussion is the new layout of the estate at Sotherton intended by Mr Rushworth. Most of those present take it for granted that 'improvements', preferably in the hands of Mr Repton, are necessary. Fanny demurs quietly to Edmund, and Edmund, although tactful about Mr Rushworth's intentions, thinks he would like to make any change to a property of his own gradually and to his own taste rather than entrust it to a professional. Henry Crawford, it seems, has some experience in 'improvements', and a visit to Sotherton by a party from those present is proposed: this is to include Henry, but omit Lady Bertram, who rarely moves from her sofa, and Fanny.

Mary Crawford announces that she is expecting the delivery from London of her harp the next day. Edmund, alternately attracted by her charm and repelled by what he considers the improper nature of some of her conversation, looks forward to hearing her play.

This is one of Jane Austen's virtuoso conversation pieces, in which the members of a large cast reveal more about themselves to the reader and the plot is advanced. Apart from the discussions mentioned above, Mrs Norris bickers with Dr Grant, Mrs Grant acts as peacemaker, Mr Rushworth boasts, and Fanny and Edmund are allied in their distrust of professional 'improvements' (see Settings for a comment on landscape gardening).

In particular, Edmund begins to be drawn under the spell of Mary Crawford, whose vivacious and sophisticated conversation nevertheless causes him concern. She shows herself to be a typical town-dweller in her failure to understand that farmers are unlikely to have a wagon free for such frivolities as the conveyance of harps at harvest time. She speaks disrespectfully of her uncle, the admiral, and makes a very coarse joke, so that Edmund 'again felt grave'.

begun in dilapidations the relationship between Mrs Norris and the Grants has begun with disagreement over the Parsonage's state of repair – the implication is that Mrs Norris's 'improvements' are a figment of her imagination and that the Parsonage was not kept in good repair
I collect I gather
Of _Rears_, and _Vices_ of rear-admirals and vice-admirals: a pun about homosexual practices in the navy

CHAPTER 7 (VOLUME I, CHAPTER vii)

Edmund neglects Fanny

Fanny and Edmund agree on the impropriety of some of Mary Crawford's conversation at dinner, but this chapter charts Edmund's growing fascination with Mary. He spends mornings and evenings at the Parsonage and Mary deploys her charms to advantage in her playing of the harp. Mary is a good and spirited horsewoman and Edmund begins to lend her what Fanny has considered 'her' mare for morning rides, leaving Fanny without her usual, much enjoyed exercise. When he finds Fanny unwell with a headache, he recollects that she has been missing her riding for the last few days, and walking too much in the heat on Mrs Norris's unnecessary errands. He is full of remorse for his neglect of his cousin.

Fanny is still far from robust, and neither a musician nor a daring rider. The extreme contrast between her and Mary Crawford is highlighted in this chapter.

tambour frame drum-shaped – i.e. circular – embroidery frame

the poor-basket a sewing basket in which fabric to be made up and partly finished garments intended for the poor were kept

CHAPTER 8 (VOLUME I, CHAPTER viii)

The journey to Sotherton; Fanny is included after all

Mr Rushworth revives the plan for a visit to Sotherton. After much arranging and re-arranging, and much to the annoyance of Mrs Norris, Edmund organises the outing so that Fanny can go after all, he staying at home to keep his mother company. Mrs Grant offers to stay with Lady Bertram, so Edmund, too, is able to go. He rides on horseback, whilst Henry Crawford drives his sister Mary, the Bertram girls, Mrs Norris and Fanny in his smart barouche. Mrs Grant prompts Julia to sit in the coveted seat next to the driver. Mary and Fanny are both absorbed in the intermittent appearances of Edmund behind the carriage on his horse; Maria is sulky and jealous until the party reaches the outskirts of her intended husband's property, after which she takes pleasure in describing some of the wonders of the Sotherton estate.

This is an amusing episode, in which emotions are both hidden and revealed: Maria and Julia are vying for Henry's attention – on this occasion Julia triumphs, to Maria's chagrin. Mary's interest in Edmund is growing, and she watches for his appearance every now and then, unaware that the feelings of Fanny beside her are deeply committed to her cousin. Mrs Norris, self-satisfied as usual, knows little of the emotional involvements of her young companions.

Jane Austen makes it possible for the reader to visualise the seating arrangements in the barouche: Henry and Julia facing forward on the driver's box; Mary and Fanny behind them, facing backwards and therefore able to catch glimpses of Edmund from time to time; Mrs Norris and Maria at the rear of the carriage, but facing forwards so that Maria is tormented by the sight of her sister and of Henry, 'full of conversation and merriment'.

Court-Leet and Court-Baron ancient rights of assembly and judicial authority

CHAPTER 9 (VOLUME I, CHAPTER ix)

The house and grounds at Sotherton

After a meal, the party is taken on a tour of the huge house and the chapel. Fanny is a little disappointed, murmuring to Edmund, 'This is not my idea of a chapel' – she had hoped for traditional qualities; instead, the interior has much less atmosphere than she expected, having been 'improved' by an earlier generation.

The chapel is no longer used for family prayers – a change for the better, in Mary Crawford's view. She makes some disparaging remarks about clergymen, and is put out when she learns that Edmund is to be ordained.

Three groups then form: Henry Crawford, Mr Rushworth and Maria; Edmund, Fanny and Mary Crawford; Mrs Rushworth, Mrs Norris and Julia. The first two groups set off to walk in the grounds, the others remain at the house. Edmund, Fanny and Mary make their way towards the wilderness, Mary still expressing her feelings about the wretchedness of a clergyman's position in society. After a while, Fanny needs to rest; the other two soon move on, leaving her alone on a seat in the wood.

Fanny's disappointment over what she sees as the mundane chapel betrays a **Romantic** streak in her feelings and in her reading. The rapport between Edmund and Fanny is clear in their quiet literary exchange, revealing shared knowledge of Romantic texts. Mary Crawford's only too candid comments demonstrate yet again her lack of discretion: her dismay at learning of Edmund's vocation and her persistence with the theme during their walk show that she is beginning to think of him as a possible husband.

window tax a tax on more than a specified number of windows in a house; in operation from the end of the seventeenth century to the middle of the nineteenth century

'blown by the night wind of Heaven' ... a 'Scottish monarch sleeps below' near quotations from Walter Scott's *The Lay of the Last Minstrel* (1805), a work of extreme Romanticism

prefer Blair's Professor the Rev. Hugh Blair (1718–1800) published five volumes of popular sermons

ha-ha a boundary ditch (see Settings)

CHAPTER 10 (VOLUME I, CHAPTER X)

Romantic wanderings

Mr Rushworth, Henry Crawford and Maria find Fanny still sitting alone on the seat and join her. The locked gate to the park is nearby and Maria expresses a desire to go through to the park. Mr Rushworth is persuaded to return to the house for the key and no sooner has he left than Maria and Crawford find their way rather perilously around the side of the gate and over the ha-ha. They disappear. Julia arrives, cross, out of breath, and dismayed to learn that Henry and Maria have gone off together. She follows them. Poor Mr Rushworth, arriving with the key, is disconcerted to find his fiancée has gone ahead and is nowhere to be seen. Fanny, trying to put the best complexion on the turn of events, assures him that the others will be waiting for him ahead and, eventually, he too sets off across the park. Fanny sets off, in turn, to search for Edmund and Mary; finally, all the members of the party reassemble in the house for dinner. Julia resumes her favoured place beside Henry Crawford on the journey home.

> The extensive grounds of Sotherton offer the opportunity for romantic games of secret walks and an escape from convention. Maria's crossing of the boundary into the park clearly conveys the idea of her crossing a moral boundary, too, in deceiving Mr Rushworth and indulging her infatuation with Crawford. (See Language and Style on the relationship of this passage to *A Midsummer Night's Dream*.)
>
> Fanny is seen at her most typical – alone and observant, having her own understanding of what is happening, but confiding in no one.

Mrs Norris's habitual self-satisfaction and lack of perception are underlined at the end of this chapter as she sets off for home smugly, with no idea of what has been happening among the young people.

I cannot get out, as the starling said an allusion to the caged starling in Laurence Sterne's *A Sentimental Journey* (1768). Some critics have noted that Mr Rushworth sees Sotherton as 'a prison – quite a dismal old prison' (p. 45) and that Maria feels the same in the light of her impending marriage

little heath heather

CHAPTER 11 (VOLUME I, CHAPTER xi)

Miss Crawford on the clergy

Sir Thomas writes that he expects to reach Mansfield Park in November. This news is received with mixed feelings by his family, his daughters not relishing the resumption of his severe regime and Maria especially dreading the fact that his return will be followed by her marriage to Mr Rushworth. The Crawfords spend the evening at Mansfield Park and Mary takes the opportunity to launch a double-pronged witty attack on the proposed marriage and on Edmund's ordination. In a conversation with Edmund and Fanny she pretends to imagine that, when Sir Thomas returns home safely from the dangers of his journey, he will – like heroes of old – offer sacrifices to the gods. Maria will be sacrificed in a loveless marriage, she implies, and Edmund will be offered up like a sacrificial victim to the Church. She suggests that young men are drawn into the Church by the lure of a comfortable living and uses her brother-in-law, Dr Grant, as an example of a clergyman who is 'an indolent selfish Bon vivant'.

She goes to join the other young people at the piano-forte, and Edmund lingers to talk with Fanny for a little, about the beautiful evening and the stars, but he is soon drawn to follow Mary.

In this exchange with Mary Crawford, Fanny speaks out in defence of Edmund and his principles. Later, alone with Edmund, she reveals her views on nature. It is clear that the cousins have studied the stars together; however, when Edmund has to choose between going out on the lawn with Fanny for further stargazing or joining Mary and the music makers, it is Mary who wins.

glee song for several voices

CHAPTER 12 (VOLUME I, CHAPTER xii)
An impromptu ball

After some months of attending race meetings and other social activities, Tom returns to Mansfield Park for the shooting season. Henry Crawford briefly visits his own estate, Everingham, in Norfolk, for the same purpose. He is soon back, however, and the opportunity arises for an impromptu ball – Fanny's first. It is an informal affair, with a fiddler from among the servants and five couples available to dance.

> The older generation watch the changing couples dancing and make mistaken comments about the happiness of Maria and the likelihood of a match being made between Julia and Henry. Fanny notices nothing but Edmund's presence when she dances with him. Tom's amusing but rather raffish style is evident, but he behaves ungallantly, dancing with his cousin only in order to avoid being drawn into a game of cards.

CHAPTER 13 (VOLUME I, CHAPTER xiii)
Mr Yates proposes family theatricals

The Hon. John Yates, a new friend among Tom's wide acquaintance, and one of whom Sir Thomas is unlikely to approve, is visiting. He has just come from a large house party, where a proposed amateur theatrical presentation has been abandoned because of a death in the family. After a casual suggestion of Tom's, he is anxious to put on a play at Mansfield Park, an idea welcomed by the Bertram girls. Edmund and Fanny are horrified, knowing that Sir Thomas would never permit such a thing. However, Tom is determined and easily persuades his mother and Mrs Norris of the value of the enterprise. The Crawfords are readily enlisted to join the cast. Fanny's only hope is that they will not be able to find a suitable play.

> Tom's wit and liveliness are demonstrated in his neat wordplay upon the titles of *Lovers' Vows* and *My Grandmother*, and his

high-handedness is evident in his promotion of a rash enterprise (see Social Background for comment on amateur theatricals). He is also the source of much comedy: he suggests to his brother that the purpose of the theatricals is to distract his mother from the terrible anxieties she is suffering over Sir Thomas's journey. This, of course, is not borne out when they look at their mother, always placid, who has 'sunk back in one corner of the sofa, the picture of health, wealth, ease, and tranquillity' and is 'just falling into a gentle doze'. The brothers laugh, but are soon involved in a heated argument. (See Textual Analysis for a detailed analysis of part of this chapter.)

My Grandmother the title of a musical farce by Prince Hoare (1794)
to be'd and *not to be'd* a reference to Shakespeare's *Hamlet*; other Shakespearean references in this chapter are to Shylock in *The Merchant of Venice*, to *Richard III* and to *Julius Caesar*
my name was Norval a reference to a popular speech in *Douglas, A Tragedy* (1757), a play by John Hoare

CHAPTER 14 (VOLUME I, CHAPTER xiv)

The play is chosen

After much discussion and argument, the play with which Yates is already familiar is settled upon. *Lovers' Vows* offers a variety of parts and both Maria and Julia are anxious to play opposite Henry Crawford. Maria secures the role and Julia, sensing her sister's complicity in this with Crawford, and failing to get the other good role, withdraws in a jealous rage from the production. Fanny silently pities her, recognising in Julia the pangs of jealousy which she herself experiences in relation to Edmund's growing attraction to Mary Crawford. Fanny reads a copy of the play, which shocks her.

Lovers' Vows is a play by the actress, novelist and dramatist Elizabeth Inchbald (1753–1851). Her version, first performed in 1798, was adapted from *Das Kind der Liebe* ('The Love Child') by the German dramatist August von Kotzebue (1761–1819), whose work was influential at the time – not least in its effect upon the English stage. The plot, briefly, concerns amongst others Agatha, who has earlier been seduced and deserted by Baron Wildenhaim.

She is discovered living in poverty by her illegitimate son, Frederick, to whom she tells the story of his birth. Although they are assisted by kind-hearted cottagers, Frederick is reduced to begging in order to help his mother; he next attempts to rob a wealthy man who is, unknown to him, his father, the Baron. All is discovered and identities revealed after his arrest. Frederick and the pastor Anhalt persuade Baron Wildenhaim to marry Agatha. The Baron's daughter, Amelia, is in love with Anhalt, who is her tutor, and is allowed to marry him instead of her wealthy suitor, Count Cassel.

What shocks Fanny in this comedy–melodrama is the fact that the leading female roles of Agatha (Maria) and Amelia (Mary Crawford) are quite improper – 'the situation of one, and the language of the other, so unfit to be expressed by any woman of modesty'. Agatha is the mother of an illegitimate son, Frederick (Henry Crawford), who she re-encounters later in life, their relationship involving many emotional scenes; Amelia has a passionate love scene with her tutor. Fanny takes rather seriously the play's total lack of decorum and promotion of extreme **Romantic** views of personal freedom. (See Language and Style for further comment on **intertextuality**.)

The many plays referred to in this chapter, some now obscure, give an indication of what was in vogue in the theatre at this time.

CHAPTER 15 (VOLUME I, CHAPTER XV)

Edmund's final attempt to stop the theatricals

Edmund is amazed to learn that *Lovers' Vows* has been thought fitting for home performance. He tries to persuade Maria against it, assuming that, once she has read it, she will be equally horrified. However, she is already familiar with the play and accepts it as perfectly suitable 'with a very few omissions, and so forth'. His appeals to his mother and aunt are similarly unsuccessful.

Work on the theatre, in the billiard room, with Sir Thomas's room next door serving as a green room, has begun. Mr Rushworth has been given a role (Count Cassel) which he does not realise will render him foolish; he is excited about his costumes, including a pink satin cape, and self-important about the lines he will have to learn. Fanny and Edmund are needed to fill remaining roles, but they express their resolution against acting. Fanny is rebuked by Mrs Norris as 'a very obstinate, ungrateful girl'. An outsider is to be brought in to play the romantic lead opposite Mary Crawford, which, she confides to Fanny, 'will be very disagreeable, and by no means what I expected'.

> Edmund and Fanny are isolated by their attitude to the play, although Fanny is as observant as ever towards what is going on around her.

> Mary Crawford comes to Fanny's aid after Mrs Norris's spiteful attack and, although Fanny never finds herself able to like Mary, not least because of Edmund's attraction to her, she is grateful. In fact, Mary has hinted on a previous occasion that she does not think Fanny is always properly treated at Mansfield Park, when she enquired as to whether she was 'out' or not (Chapter 5).

> Mrs Norris reveals her liking for small-scale economies in her triumphant account of her defeat of a small boy, son of an estate carpenter, who had apparently hoped to get a free dinner in the servants' hall. She is meanwhile fully enjoying the extravagant preparation of the theatre.

CHAPTER 16 (VOLUME I, CHAPTER XVi)

Edmund is persuaded

Fanny finds solace in what has come to be called 'her' room, the old schoolroom, which is now known as the East room. Here she keeps her books and a few plants; the furnishings are plain, but evocative of the girls' earlier years; gifts from members of the family, especially Tom, make her feel guilty about her refusal to join in his theatrical venture. Mrs Norris has instructed that a fire must not be lit for Fanny's benefit (and this has never been countermanded), but she likes to retire here, where Edmund has often joined her and guided her reading. He arrives to discuss what he has already decided – that he will take the romantic lead opposite Mary Crawford, in spite of his previous resolution against acting. This is to spare Mary the unpleasantness of acting with a stranger.

Fanny, knowing that the role will involve Edmund in love scenes with Mary, is deeply disturbed by this change, although she cannot bring herself to say so. She blames it on Mary's influence.

Fanny is seen against a different background here. Although Edmund plays the role of Fanny's guide and adviser, it is becoming clear that it is he who needs Fanny's approval at this point in the narrative. The books she has out to read are looked at by Edmund, and reveal her taste and the fact that her reading is up to date. *Crabbe's Tales* came out in 1812, and is often used as a device to establish the chronology of the novel. The scenes depicted in the transparencies (Tintern Abbey, an Italian cave and a moonlit lake) reflect Fanny's interest in **Romantic** subjects.

transparencies pictures seen when the light passes through them, often presented at that time on oiled paper or finely woven linen
the Idler a series of essays (1758–60) by Dr Samuel Johnson (one of Fanny's favourite authors) contributed to *The Universal Chronicle or Weekly Gazette*

CHAPTER 17 (VOLUME I, CHAPTER xvii)

Fanny is anxious; Julia is unhappy

Edmund's submission to the will of the others is seen as a triumph, while Edmund is happy that Mary Crawford is so pleased to play opposite him. In fact all are happy and busy, except Fanny and Julia. Julia is jealous of Henry Crawford's by now obvious preference for her sister. Mrs Grant is worried by this involvement of her half-brother with an engaged girl, especially when Mary says to. her 'I would not give much for Mr. Rushworth's chance, if Henry stept in before the articles were signed.' Mrs Grant determines to speak to Henry after the play is finished. Julia's misery goes unremarked by her family, all absorbed in their roles, except for Fanny, who knows how Julia is suffering; Fanny is concerned, too, that Edmund has ultimately put aside his principles so willingly.

Fanny is on her own, the principled alliance with Edmund ended, as he now finds himself 'between love and consistency', as his feelings for Mary intensify.

address to Tobacco Mary Crawford shows her quick wit in parodying Isaac Hawkins Browne's work *A Pipe of Tobacco: in Imitation of Six Several Authors* (1736), itself a series of pastiches

CHAPTER 18 (VOLUME I, CHAPTER xviii)

Rehearsals – and an interruption

Progress is made with *Lovers' Vows* but, to Edmund's dismay, Tom's plans grow ever grander, with a scene painter arriving from London and invitations issued to all Tom's local acquaintances, instead of keeping the entertainment within a slightly expanded family group.

Fanny finds a role as sympathetic listener to the various complaints of the participants, and is the only person prepared to help the inadequate Mr Rushworth learn his lines. His earlier jealousy of Maria's liking for Henry returns, as it becomes obvious even to his limited understanding that their endlessly repeated rehearsals together are opportunistic rather than necessary.

One morning, first Mary and then Edmund seek out Fanny in the East room, to ask her to hear their lines. She is made miserable as she listens to their spirited rendering of a love scene.

Before the first full rehearsal in the evening, Dr Grant is taken ill and Mrs Grant is unable to play the part of Cottager's Wife. Even Fanny bows to pressure and agrees to play the small part which, like much of the play, she already knows from helping others to rehearse. However, as the full-scale rehearsal gets under way, Julia comes in 'aghast' to break the news that Sir Thomas, returned unexpectedly early, is in the house.

The details of the final preparations for the performance of the play are built up and even the previously determined Fanny is drawn in. The final chapter of Volume I ends with a dramatic climax, which is going to lead to many difficult explanations to the returning head of the house.

festoons theatre curtains of the period were drawn up in the style to be seen today in what are called 'Austrian' blinds

VOLUME II

CHAPTER 19 (VOLUME II, CHAPTER i)

Sir Thomas discovers the theatre

The members of the horror-struck assembly pull themselves together; Tom, Edmund, Maria and Mr Rushworth go to the drawing room to meet Sir Thomas. Fanny is left with the Crawfords and John Yates. The Crawfords, who recognise the nature of the crisis, slip away home to the Parsonage. Yates declines to leave with them. When Fanny goes to join the rest of the family in the drawing room, she is moved by Sir Thomas's unusual kindness and real pleasure in seeing her again – improved in looks and health, as he believes her to be. The moment of revelation is postponed as Sir Thomas gives the family an account of his travels.

However, when Sir Thomas goes to his room, he finds it disturbed; in the billiard room next door he comes upon Yates, a stranger to him, delivering his lines on the recently erected stage. Later, the insensitive Yates gives a full account of the theatrical venture to an ever graver Sir Thomas, who looks reproachfully at his family – and particularly so at Edmund, upon whose good sense he has relied. Mr Rushworth (discreetly relieved of his pink cloak by Mrs Norris) creates an unexpectedly favourable impression upon his future father-in-law when he expresses his distaste for the play.

> The discomfort of Sir Thomas's children becomes more and more acute as they realise how seriously displeased he will be by their activities in his absence; they know, too, that he will put an end to the whole project. There is considerable comedy in the situation as well – not least in Lady Bertram's total unawareness of anything untoward and of course in the first meeting on stage between the master of the house and Yates, who later totally fails to see that his eager account of the production is received more and more discouragingly by Sir Thomas.

> There is **irony**, too, in the contrast between the dramatic exaggerations of the play in which the younger people are involved and the real dangers of travel in the early nineteenth century –

particularly in a time of war – to which Sir Thomas has been exposed.

a French privateer an armed, independent ship commissioned by the French government to attack enemy vessels – a hazard to British ships during the Napoleonic Wars

CHAPTER 20 (VOLUME II, CHAPTER ii)

Decorum prevails

Edmund explains events to his father, praising Fanny for her persistent resistance to the play, which she recognised would be against the wishes of Sir Thomas. Mrs Norris has the unfamiliar experience of hearing remonstrations from her brother-in-law about her failure to guide the young people aright. Yates at last understands that he is to be disappointed once again in his theatrical expectations. Maria's hopes that Henry Crawford's obvious admiration of her would proceed to a proposal of marriage are dashed; his departure – for an indefinite stay at Bath – is followed shortly by that of Yates.

> Although Sir Thomas had encouraged some acting when his sons were children, his distaste for adult domestic theatricals is well understood by his family; to outsiders it is perhaps baffling, since it takes some time for Yates to recognise that the return of the master of Mansfield Park has put an end to the production. Henry Crawford, too, envisages a possible resumption of rehearsals. The theatricals, in fact, mark a clear-cut division in the novel between those opposed, who are seen as principled, and those for, who are seen as infected with a taste for worldly and improper pleasures. (See Social Background for comment on amateur theatricals.)

> Mrs Norris for once is caught in the wrong. Sir Thomas has lost confidence in her judgement, although she is astute enough to turn aside his disapproval for the moment by boasting of her hard work in bringing about the match between Maria and Mr Rushworth.

CHAPTER 21 (VOLUME II, CHAPTER iii)

Maria marries

A dullness descends upon Mansfield Park in contrast to the excitement of the previous weeks; only the serious Fanny enjoys a return to the former quietness. Edmund tells an embarrassed Fanny that her uncle finds her 'very pretty' and says teasingly: 'You must really begin to harden yourself to the idea of being worth looking at.—You must try not to mind growing up into a pretty woman.'

After a visit to Sotherton, Sir Thomas is dismayed by Mr Rushworth's inadequacies as a husband for his daughter. He questions Maria as to her real feelings for Rushworth. Maria, accepting that she has lost Henry Crawford, claims that this marriage is all that she desires. The wedding takes place with due regard to 'the etiquette of the day' and the couple leave for Brighton, Julia accompanying her sister.

> Maria's bitter marriage of material convenience strikes a harsh note and prepares the reader for impending difficulties in that quarter.

> Fanny asks her uncle about the slave trade in this chapter. An Act of Parliament abolishing the slave trade was passed in 1807, and it seems likely that Fanny was asking Sir Thomas about progress in this matter. This passage (pp. 165–6), although brief, has attracted much attention from critics interested in placing early novels in their historical context (see Recent Criticism).

CHAPTER 22 (VOLUME II, CHAPTER iv)

Fanny and Mary

Her cousins having left, Fanny is the only young woman remaining at Mansfield Park and, as such, finds herself of more consequence than before. She is welcome, too, at the Parsonage, where Mary Crawford is finding life dull. Their acquaintance ripens, although Fanny is unable to develop affection for her neighbour, aware as she is of Edmund's feelings for Mary. Fanny always senses Mary's cynicism, although sometimes enjoying, against her better judgement, Mary's humorous lack of respect for others.

A meeting in the grounds of the Parsonage between the two women and Edmund gives Mary Crawford the opportunity to declare that she intends to marry a wealthy man: that is, not a clergyman. Edmund's hopes are also made clear. Edmund and Fanny are invited by Mrs Grant to dine at the Parsonage the next day.

Fanny's sufferings at having to witness Edmund's ever-increasing passion for Mary Crawford continue, but she is seen as gaining in character and confidence as her circumstances become more pleasant.

An amusing contrast between Fanny and Mary is offered as they sit in the shrubbery: Fanny offers two speeches which sound somewhat rehearsed – the first combining some philosophical ideas about landscape gardening and memory, the second commenting on the beauties of nature. Mary does not respond at all to the first, and to the second she replies, like a town-lover, that the only wonder she feels in the shrubbery is like that said to have been expressed by a Doge at Versailles: as being unequal to his wonder at finding himself there. Mary's wit and sophistication – although superficial – are particularly marked in relation to Fanny's inexperience and touchingly naïve attempts at serious conversation.

myrtle and turkey products of the nurseryman and poulterer mentioned by Mary Crawford and Mrs Grant. The myrtle has a white, scented flower and is traditionally dedicated to Venus

CHAPTER 23 (VOLUME II, CHAPTER V)

Fanny goes out to dine

Lady Bertram and Mrs Norris are surprised that Fanny should be asked to dine without the family at the Parsonage and are disinclined to let her go. On Edmund's representations, however, Sir Thomas approves the visit. Mrs Norris is spiteful and insists that Fanny should walk but Sir Thomas, as a matter of course, orders the carriage for her. Fanny relishes her new opportunity and is moved by Sir Thomas's kindness to her. She will be able to wear the spotted white dress that he bought for her as a bridesmaid at Maria's wedding. Nevertheless, she dreads having to see

Edmund and Mary together and is distressed to find that Henry Crawford has returned to the Parsonage.

The date of Edmund's ordination is drawing near, and Mary – who had hoped to influence him against his vocation – is vexed.

> Fanny's dislike and distrust of Henry Crawford increase as he speaks rather coarsely of Rushworth and his bride and hints at a liaison between Julia and Yates.

menus plaisirs (French: 'little pleasures') pocket or pin money

CHAPTER 24 (VOLUME II, CHAPTER vi)

Henry Crawford turns his affections towards Fanny; William visits

Henry has observed Fanny's increasing good looks and tells his sister that he intends to make Fanny fall in love with him. Mary says that Fanny is no different, just better dressed and the only young woman available in whom he could be interested. She realises that Fanny's coldness towards her brother is a challenge to him.

William's ship, the *Antwerp*, finally arrives at Portsmouth and Sir Thomas invites him to visit. William, after seven years in the navy, impresses his uncle, and Fanny is overjoyed to find that she and her brother are as fond of each other as ever. William has many adventures to relate and is popular with all at Mansfield Park, as well as with Henry Crawford, who lends him a horse for the duration of his visit.

> Henry's efforts to ingratiate himself with Fanny, not least by his interest in her brother's exploits, are not entirely unsuccessful. Fanny's reunion with her brother brings her news of the family with which she is out of touch.

disesteem indifferent regard

CHAPTER 25 (VOLUME II, CHAPTER vii)

An evening at the Parsonage

The Bertrams, with Mrs Norris, Fanny and William, dine at the Parsonage; Sir Thomas has become aware of Crawford's interest in

Fanny and accepts the invitation, partly to promote the possibility of a highly desirable match being made for Fanny. The evening is successful, with Henry taking advantage of the game of Speculation to sit between Fanny and the vague Lady Bertram. He makes suggestions to Edmund about improvements to the property in which he is to live, after ordination, at Thornton Lacey. Both Fanny and Mary Crawford are interested in this topic. William complains to his sister that he seems to have no prospect of promotion in the navy.

> A lengthy chapter which again demonstrates Jane Austen's skilful control of conversation amongst a large cast of characters. The account of the evening allows for the development of several strands of the plot, as well as further understandings and misunderstandings between various members of the party. The game of Speculation to a certain extent **symbolises** the 'state of play' of the characters' various relationships at this point in the narrative, while the individual characteristics of the players are revealed by their reactions to the game.

> **Speculation**   a card game, in which players gamble for notional wealth

CHAPTER 26 (VOLUME II, CHAPTER viii)

Sir Thomas plans a ball; the amber cross

Sir Thomas decides to give a ball for his niece and nephew at Mansfield Park – much to the horror of the ever detestable Mrs Norris, whose imagined organisational skills are now seen by Sir Thomas for the interfering nuisance that they are. He in fact makes the plans for the dance himself. Fanny intends to wear an amber cross given to her by William. It has no chain, as the additional expense was beyond William's means; at the Parsonage Mary Crawford persuades Fanny to choose a gold necklace to carry the cross, as a present from a selection which she offers. Fanny is dismayed to find that the necklace she reluctantly picks out was one bought by Henry Crawford.

> Mary Crawford's collusion with her brother in tricking Fanny into accepting his necklace is guessed at by Fanny – Mary sees this, and she deviously pre-empts Fanny by asking if she suspects 'a confederacy', thereby making it impossible for Fanny to say

so, due to social considerations of politeness. (See Language and Style for a comment on the **symbolism** surrounding the cross and chains; see also Jane Austen's Life for a parallel incident in which Jane and her sister were given topaz crosses by a sailor brother.)

Mrs Norris's influence in the family, on the wane since Sir Thomas's return from Antigua, reaches a new low as she is foiled in her attempts to become involved in the organisation of the ball.

coze comfortable chat (probably from French *causerie* – 'informal conversation' – with added sense from 'cosy')

CHAPTER 27 (VOLUME II, CHAPTER ix)

Fanny prepares for the ball

On her return from the Parsonage, Fanny discovers Edmund has thoughtfully bought her a gold chain himself – it is plain and more suited to the amber cross. Edmund persuades her with some difficulty that it would not be courteous to return the necklace to the Crawfords, and that she must wear it at the ball.

Henry's attentions to William continue. In anticipation of William's leaving to rejoin his ship after the ball, Henry invites William to travel 'post' with him in his hired carriage (rather than with the less comfortable 'mail' or public coach), and to meet his uncle, the admiral.

On the day of the ball, Edmund – who is to leave to prepare for ordination the next day – confides in Fanny that Mary has said she will never marry a clergyman, although she has agreed to dance with him. Mary, too, is expected to leave soon, for London. Edmund, hitherto optimistic, now sees his hopes of marriage to Mary receding; yet he also expresses once again his anxieties about her, fearing that not only her manner but her mind is 'tainted'.

To Fanny's relief, the cross will not fit on the Crawfords' necklace, and she wears it on Edmund's chain. Feeling happy and satisfied with her appearance, she wears the necklace as well. Too late, Lady Bertram sends her personal maid to help Fanny dress for the ball.

Fanny's status in the household continues to improve: not only is a ball to be held for her and William, but Lady Bertram has thought of sending her assistance so that she might look her best on this grand occasion. The maid arrives too late, of course, but the intention is there, as well as the recognition, at last, of Fanny as a young woman of some consequence in the family.

When Edmund confides in Fanny his doubts about his prospects with Mary Crawford, she hears this with some relief. She shows her sensitivity, however, in warning Edmund against speaking to her disparagingly about Mary's qualities: she can see that this could be embarrassing should Edmund and Mary eventually come together. Edmund's dependence on Fanny is increasing.

CHAPTER 28 (VOLUME II, CHAPTER X)

Fanny is admired

Fanny looks well at the ball and survives the formalities of introductions and the frightening honour of opening the ball with Henry Crawford as her dancing partner. She is generally admired. Her enjoyment of the evening is mixed: Mary Crawford's continuing interest in Edmund disturbs her, while Henry Crawford's attentions give her no satisfaction. The fatigue that comes over her after dancing with Edmund means that she goes to bed 'early' at three in the morning.

This is rather like a scene from the traditional story of Cinderella, in which the retiring and unknown Miss Price 'comes out', if not absolutely as the belle of the ball, at least as an attractive young woman with a position in society as the niece of Sir Thomas. To all but Fanny, Henry Crawford may well seem to fit the role of Prince Charming.

à-la-mortal mixed, like all human experience
the Lady of Branxholm Hall from Walter Scott's *The Lay of the Last Minstrel* (1805), drawing an amusingly exaggerated comparison between Fanny and a dangerous medieval heroine. *The Lay of the Last Minstrel* is also alluded to in Chapter 9

CHAPTER 29 (VOLUME II, CHAPTER xi)

Departures

After the excitement of the ball, Fanny has to get up early for breakfast, when she says goodbye to her brother, who leaves with Henry Crawford. He is followed soon afterwards by Edmund, who goes to Peterborough to his friends, the Owens, where he will prepare for his ordination. Lady Bertram has grown greatly to value Fanny's company, with her two daughters away from home (they have meanwhile left Brighton for London). Mary Crawford awaits the return of her brother to the Parsonage after which they, too, expect to leave Mansfield. Mary is anxious to see Edmund, now staying longer than expected with the Owens, before she goes to London. She cross-questions Fanny about the grown-up Owen daughters, fearing that Edmund is attracted to one of them.

> Fanny's confidence continues to grow and she bears the departure of the two people dearest to her – William and Edmund – better than she had hoped.

con amore (Italian) with love

CHAPTER 30 (VOLUME II, CHAPTER xii)

Henry plans to marry Fanny

Henry Crawford, on his return to Mansfield, astonishes his sister by insisting that he has gone far beyond his inclination towards a flirtation with Fanny, and has now decided to marry her. After she has recovered from her surprise, Mary – who thinks well of Fanny, in spite of her lack of fortune – assumes that Fanny will of course agree.

> Henry Crawford shows the better side of his character in his appreciation of Fanny's qualities and in his intention to make her happy.

the pleasing plague a description of love in the eighteenth-century Poet Laureate William Whitehead's 'The Je ne scai Quoi. A Song'

CHAPTER 31 (VOLUME II, CHAPTER xiii)

William promoted; Henry refused

Henry Crawford calls at Mansfield Park and soon has an opportunity to speak to Fanny alone. He brings news of her brother's promotion to lieutenant, as a result of the recommendation of Admiral Crawford, to whom Henry had introduced William. In spite of Fanny's gratitude to Henry on her brother's behalf, she is distraught when he begins to speak to her of marriage and she runs away.

A note from Mary Crawford, congratulating her on the supposed engagement, makes Fanny even more disturbed. Later, in the evening, when others are present, Henry's attentions to her become yet more marked. He persuades her to respond to Mary's letter, which she does in dismissive terms, hoping that this will bring the matter to a conclusion.

> The reader is not surprised when the Crawfords' confident expectation of success is thwarted. Fanny's earlier shocked observation of Henry's duplicitous behaviour to Maria and Julia has developed into a confirmed disapproval of his character.

> Although Volume II ends with Fanny hoping that she has dismissed Henry Crawford's proposal once and for all, the reader guesses that he will not be dissuaded so easily.

VOLUME III

CHAPTER 32 (VOLUME III, CHAPTER i)

Sir Thomas is stern

Fanny hopes that she has made her feelings clear to the Crawfords, but Sir Thomas comes to the East room bearing what he believes to be delightful news: he has had a visit from Mr Crawford, requesting his approval to the proposed marriage. Sir Thomas is astonished and uncomprehending as Fanny tries to explain that she will never accept Henry. Fanny, on her side, is utterly dismayed that she should be considered selfish and ungrateful by her uncle, who – especially recently – has been so kind and considerate to her. (He had been shocked, for instance, on entering the East room to see that she had no fire, and ordered a reversal of Mrs Norris's ban on heating for Fanny.)

Fanny refuses to go down to see Henry Crawford herself and her uncle, noticing that her tears have spoilt her looks, goes himself. He returns in a more temperate mood, believing that Fanny will respond to kindly persistence, praising Mr Crawford's forbearance and insisting that Fanny must see him herself soon. After a walk in the shrubbery to compose herself, and an attack on her character by Mrs Norris at dinner, Fanny is summoned to Sir Thomas's room, where Henry is waiting for her.

> In both the second and third volumes, the first chapter begins with Sir Thomas being put out. Fanny shared his views on the occasion of his discovery of the amateur dramatics; now she is unhappily opposed to her guardian, whose good opinion she has lately been enjoying. He was soon able to put the situation to rights on the first occasion; now he believes that reason and continuing pressure will persuade Fanny to accept a match of which he can be proud. His estimation of Fanny's worth obviously rises even higher as the highly eligible Mr Crawford seeks her hand.

CHAPTER 33 (VOLUME III, CHAPTER ii)

Henry Crawford tries again

To Fanny's despair, Henry Crawford persists in his attachment to her, and her uncle agrees that he should continue to call whilst at Mansfield. They believe that she will be won by persistence. Her aunts are told of the situation by Sir Thomas: Mrs Norris, forbidden by her brother-in-law to speak about the matter, is angry and begrudges Fanny what she sees as her success; Lady Bertram looks on Fanny with a new respect, expressing her view that 'it is every young woman's duty to accept such a very unexceptionable offer as this.' She even offers Fanny a puppy from Pug's next litter.

> Fanny is unable to make anyone see that her mind is made up against Henry Crawford's proposal. The aunts react typically: Mrs Norris, though silent, with obvious ill will towards Fanny; Lady

Bertram discovering an unexpected new kinship with Fanny – that of one admired beauty with another. Lady Bertram echoes the word 'duty' – used of Maria's thoughts earlier in the narrative (p. 34) – in relation to marriage. She congratulates herself yet again on having sent her maid to help Fanny dress on the night of the ball when, she believes, Henry must have fallen in love with Fanny.

CHAPTER 34 (VOLUME III, CHAPTER iii)

Henry Crawford takes centre stage

Edmund, returning late from the Owens after ordination, is surprised to find Mary Crawford still at Mansfield and to be warmly received by her. He is less surprised than his father by Fanny's refusal of Crawford, but sees Henry as a valued friend and hopes his persistence will be rewarded.

Henry Crawford has some success in interesting Fanny at an evening gathering. The opportunity arises for him to read aloud from Shakespeare's *Henry VIII*; this he does with a mastery admired by all, even Fanny. The reader is reminded how his acting 'had first taught Fanny what pleasure a play might give' in relation to the ill-fated *Lovers' Vows*. He then talks feelingly with Edmund about the need for clergymen to read well in church. Henry's charm is well displayed on this occasion – his recognised acting skills are put to good use. However, an opportunity, in which Edmund colludes, for Henry to speak privately with Fanny, ends in nothing but her vexation. Responding sharply for once, she speaks of his unusual moment of self-knowledge earlier, when he said that he would not like to be a clergyman 'for a constancy'.

The discussion on reading aloud between the two young men reflects the importance of this activity in a cultivated household.

That Crawford is able to read well so many parts in *Henry VIII* (the King, the Queen, Buckingham, Wolsey and Cromwell) demonstrates not only his acting skills but also his volatile nature – wishing he were a sailor, for instance, when talking to William, or a London clergyman when in discussion with Edmund.

CHAPTER 35 (VOLUME III, CHAPTER iv)

Edmund and Fanny

Sir Thomas enlists Edmund's assistance to persuade Fanny to look favourably on Henry Crawford's suit. The cousins have a long talk in which Fanny is able to unburden herself of her doubts about Henry's integrity and her lack of love for him. She speaks of a woman's inability to choose with whom she might fall in love and says how inappropriate it would have previously been considered for her to imagine that she might marry above her material expectations. Edmund is understanding but it is clear that he believes Henry will eventually prevail.

Edmund himself is full of hope that Mary Crawford, in spite of her often stated objections to clergymen, is still attracted to him.

> No one, least of all Edmund himself, is aware that Fanny is in love with her cousin and that this is the greatest stumbling block of all to a possible marriage with Henry Crawford.

CHAPTER 36 (VOLUME III, CHAPTER v)

The Crawfords leave for London

Before the Crawfords depart for their postponed return to London, Fanny is obliged to meet Mary Crawford for the first time since Henry's unwanted proposal. Mary uses her considerable powers of persuasion on her brother's behalf and makes clear her continuing interest in Edmund. Fanny is relieved that Mary is not angry with her, but is pleased that the Crawfords are to leave. Not believing in the constancy of Henry's devotion to her, she is left 'hoping she might never see him again till he were the husband of some other woman'.

> Fanny is unmoved by almost everything that Mary can find to say in favour of Henry, although she warms to Mary's more principled remarks about family life – contradicted almost at once, however, by her familiar view that most marriages are unhappy. We also see Mary's manipulative conversational technique when she deliberately makes a 'push at Fanny's feelings' by mentioning William's promotion, the recollection of which

is to Fanny 'the most powerful disturber of every decision against Mr. Crawford'.

the Blues the Royal Horse Guards

CHAPTER 37 (VOLUME III, CHAPTER vi)

A visit to Portsmouth is suggested

William, now Second Lieutenant on HMS *Thrush*, pays another visit to Mansfield Park. Sir Thomas, who has kept his promise not to speak of Henry Crawford's proposal, makes a plan which he hopes will further his wish for Fanny to marry. It is suggested that Fanny should return to Portsmouth with William for a visit of two or three months, to the family she has not seen since she left, aged ten, for Northamptonshire.

Fanny is delighted at the prospect, imagining a warm welcome, and receives an affectionate note from her mother before leaving. Lady Bertram is quite disconsolate, realising how much she will miss her niece. William and Fanny have an unpleasant surprise when it appears that Mrs Norris proposes to go with them; fortunately, her well-established dislike of spending her own money prevents this, since she would have to pay her own fare back to Mansfield.

> The worldly-wise Sir Thomas believes that Fanny's return to the relative poverty of her natural home will encourage her to think seriously of the advantages of a wealthy marriage.

CHAPTER 38 (VOLUME III, CHAPTER vii)

Fanny goes to Portsmouth

The arduous journey over, Fanny's feelings are mixed as she finds herself in a home much smaller and more inconvenient than she had remembered. The family are preoccupied by the impending departure of William's ship and, although most greet her, her arrival arouses little of the emotional excitement she might have expected. The boys, and particularly her father, are all concerned with what seems important to them – the navy, the movement of ships and nautical matters generally in Portsmouth. William and Mr Price enjoy an animated conversation along these lines, which means nothing to Fanny, before her father even notices her presence.

At last some tea and bread and butter is brought for the exhausted traveller; Fanny looks on, upset, as her two sisters quarrel over a silver knife left to the older one, Susan, by another sister, Mary, who died whilst Fanny was away. Betsey, the youngest daughter, seems to be her mother's favourite. Mrs Price is little interested in accounts of her family in Northamptonshire, dwelling instead on the inadequacies of her servants, which Fanny cannot fail to notice herself. She goes off to the tiny bedroom she is to share with Susan, 'leaving all below in confusion and noise', and thinking wistfully already of her little attic room at Mansfield Park.

> The contrast is great between the elegance and orderliness of Mansfield Park and the poor housekeeping, thoughtless manners, noise and general discomfort of the Portsmouth house.

> Mr Price's speech to William about nautical matters and landmarks around Portsmouth is generally believed to be accurate, and probably relies in part on advice from Jane Austen's sailor brothers. The editor of the selected text points out that the 1816 edition had some variations at this point, however.

prize money the reward shared by a crew, according to rank, following the capture of an enemy ship

Indiaman a cargo-carrying ship, trading with India

CHAPTER 39 (VOLUME III, CHAPTER viii)

Fanny in exile

Fanny's disappointment deepens: William has to set sail at once and she had hoped to have some time with him in Portsmouth. Furthermore, she finds herself unable to respect her parents. Her mother, in particular (like her sister Lady Bertram in looks and indolence, although without her means), finds her household unmanageable and shows no deepening affection for Fanny after welcoming her. Fanny feels her brothers and sisters are beyond any help or guidance she might give, except for Susan and, to some extent, Sam, whose outfit she helps to sew before he, too, goes to sea.

Within a week of arrival, Fanny is comparing Portsmouth with Mansfield Park, very much to the former's disadvantage. Not robust, she finds the constant noise at Portsmouth especially wearing.

Dr. Johnson's celebrated judgment 'Marriage has many pains, but celibacy has no pleasures', from Samuel Johnson's *The History of Rasselas, Prince of Abissinia* (1759)

CHAPTER 40 (VOLUME III, CHAPTER ix)

News from London; a sympathetic sister

Fanny finds unexpected pleasure in receiving a letter from Mary Crawford, even though the contents relating to Henry and to Edmund give her some concern. She is pleased to be reminded of the civilised society she has recently left.

She finds no friends in the limited Portsmouth society to which she is introduced, although she has a growing respect for her sister, Susan. They work together in the room they share and Fanny subscribes to a circulating library so that they can have the pleasure of reading.

A letter from her Aunt Bertram, with whom she is in regular correspondence, informs Fanny that Edmund has left for London.

Fanny believes that Edmund has gone to London to propose to Mary Crawford and from this point she dreads the arrival of the postman, who might bring her news of Edmund's engagement.

Mary's mention of 'Baron Wildenhaim' is a useful reminder to the reader of John Yates, who now reappears in the story.

CHAPTER 41 (VOLUME III, CHAPTER x)

Fanny has an unexpected visitor

As Fanny is worrying over what might have happened during the week that Edmund has been in London, an unexpected visitor calls at the Prices' house – Henry Crawford. He is as charming as ever and tactful in his dealings with her parents. He praises William in Mrs Price's presence and later, meeting Mr Price whilst out for a walk with Fanny and Susan, Henry agrees to his suggestion that they tour the dockyard.

Fanny is deeply embarrassed by her family, although things pass off better than she had hoped, with her mother and father both behaving civilly towards Crawford. The horror of his attendance at a family dinner party is avoided, much to Fanny's relief, since the squalor of her home life is most evident at mealtimes. Fanny finds Henry Crawford much improved, not least in the propriety of his attentions to her young sister and in his taking an interest in the affairs of his Norfolk estate, previously so often neglected.

Poor Fanny is thoroughly confused. Her view of Henry Crawford certainly softens, as her uncle had anticipated. His constancy seems evident, and his approach 'more gentle, obliging, and attentive to other people's feelings' than she has seen before. Her parents manage to present themselves as acceptably well-mannered, in a style not evident in everyday matters. It is clear that the manners in the Portsmouth household are adapted to suit the occasion; this contrasts with the consistently courteous, if formidable, style of Sir Thomas Bertram.

CHAPTER 42 (VOLUME III, CHAPTER xi)

Henry makes some progress

The following day, Henry Crawford joins the Prices on their way to the garrison chapel. The family, all handsome and in their Sunday clothes, look their best. Fanny and Henry, with the rest of the family, enjoy a pleasant walk on the ramparts, their sensibilities well matched in enjoyment of the views and the sunny March day.

Henry Crawford, finding that Fanny is only half-way through the planned two-month visit, and thinking that she is not finding Portsmouth good for her health, offers to escort her back to Mansfield with his sister, should she wish to go. He attempts to detain her in a private interview, talking about his plans to pay closer attention to the claims of his estate at Everingham. After their farewells, he goes off to 'the best dinner that a capital inn afforded' whilst Fanny goes indoors to the unappetising fare offered in the Price household.

Fanny feels more isolated than ever when Crawford leaves. His developing interest in his estate and his tenants, as well as his restraint in conversation with her, make her believe that his improvement is genuine.

Henry's campaign to win Fanny's hand seems to be showing signs of possible success. Fanny is quite unwell, not least because of the lack of suitable exercise; the Prices' diet seems suited to bring up sturdy children, but Fanny's refined taste, learned at Mansfield, leaves her unable to eat adequately.

Fanny does not realise that her present discomfort at Portsmouth gives an added attraction to Henry Crawford and the life he could offer, just as Sir Thomas had so shrewdly planned.

CHAPTER 43 (VOLUME III, CHAPTER xii)

A letter from Mary Crawford

A letter from Mary shows that Edmund has not yet proposed to her, although she writes warmly of him, and Fanny believes that eventually they will marry. Mary is preventing her brother from attending to his estate duties, as he had intended, because of an impending party. The sympathetic relationship between Fanny and her sister Susan continues to develop. Fanny realises that Susan is very like herself, although not shy, and she is reluctant for Susan to grow up in the unsuitable Portsmouth home.

Mary's letter shows her vivacity and the shallowness of her thinking. She is amusing and lively, but Fanny is shocked that Mary records approval of Edmund which relates only to his handsome appearance.

Henry's failure to leave for his estate, in order to attend a party, will later prove to have been a turning point with far-reaching consequences.

Jane Austen uses correspondence to solve the narrative problems which arise with her heroine isolated in Portsmouth (see Narrative Modes on the **epistolary novel**).

CHAPTER 44 (VOLUME III, CHAPTER xiii)

More correspondence; bad news

Fanny receives a long and anguished letter from Edmund. His problems remain the same: he is too much in love with Mary to give her up, but distressed by her lack of principle and her pleasure in society, which he considers unworthy. Her friends, he says, 'have been leading her astray for years'. He has returned to Mansfield and may well write to Mary in London. Giving other news, he speaks highly of Henry and the sincerity of his feelings for Fanny; he also mentions that he witnessed a meeting between Henry and Mrs Rushworth (Maria), when she responded very coldly to Henry. Dr and Mrs Grant are about to depart for Bath, leaving no one home at the Parsonage. To Fanny's disappointment, Edmund also writes to say that, although Fanny is very much missed at Mansfield, it will not be possible for Sir Thomas to fetch her until after Easter.

Another letter arrives – from Lady Bertram – with the news that Tom's excesses, particularly in drinking, have led to his serious illness. Edmund goes to fetch his brother, and Lady Bertram's next letter expresses grave concern at Tom's appearance.

> Maria Rushworth's reaction to Henry Crawford perhaps reflects some still-present raw emotions, and the reader wonders whether this will result in his seeing yet another romantic challenge.

CHAPTER 45 (VOLUME III, CHAPTER xiv)

Fanny longs for Mansfield Park

Fanny learns from a letter from Edmund that, although Lady Bertram has not been told, Tom's condition is considered serious. Fanny longs to return to Mansfield Park, but Easter passes and no date is set, since Sir Thomas does not want to leave his son. She realises fully that Mansfield Park is her true home and she particularly misses the spring season in Northamptonshire. She wishes she could be of use herself and is surprised that neither Maria nor Julia has returned to comfort Lady Bertram.

Another letter – inappropriately light-hearted – arrives from Mary Crawford. She makes it clear that, were Tom to die, leaving his brother as heir, Edmund would become a much more desirable marriage partner, even though he is a clergyman. She also mentions that Maria, whose husband has gone to Bath to fetch his mother, is spending some time with friends in Twickenham. Henry, it appears, is visiting neighbouring Richmond. Fanny declines Mary's offer to escort her home to Mansfield Park together with Henry. She is even more shocked than usual by the tone of the letter and, in any case, does not wish to act without Sir Thomas's approval.

> Fanny's emotions, though hidden, are powerful enough, but she is not a heroine who initiates action. Her passivity is given added emphasis at this point in the narrative, as events unfold at a distance from her.

> **'With what intense desire she wants her home'** a variation on a line about a homesick schoolboy from William Cowper's *Tirocinium: or, A Review of Schools* (1785)

CHAPTER 46 (VOLUME III, CHAPTER XV)

A rumour and its confirmation; Edmund takes Fanny 'home'

Half expecting another letter from Mary urging her to return to Mansfield Park with the Crawfords, Fanny is alarmed when the next letter, written in haste, is about a current rumour. This relates to Henry Crawford and, presumably, to Maria. Julia has left London – to go to Mansfield Park with Henry and Maria, Mary hopes. Mary says that she expects matters to be 'all hushed up'. Fanny is bewildered and even more alarmed when her father shows her a relevant item of gossip in his newspaper, mentioning the newly-wed 'Mrs. R.' and the 'well known and captivating Mr. C.', who have run away together. Although Fanny discounts the story to her father, she is unable to believe it untrue herself: it seems perfectly possible that Henry Crawford's vanity and Maria's attraction to him have provoked them to this dreadfully immoral behaviour.

Fanny, suffering, hears nothing further until the third day brings a letter from Edmund, who is in London with Sir Thomas. Edmund confirms their worst fears, and adds that Julia, too, has eloped – she has gone to Scotland with Yates. Lady Bertram even more desperately needs Fanny to be with her and Edmund is to fetch her the following morning. Sir Thomas, who is 'not overpowered' according to Edmund, is in fact able to give a thought to Fanny and the Prices' situation and invites Susan to return with her sister.

Fanny's delight at the prospect of returning to what she now knows to be her real 'home', and at seeing Edmund again, is mixed with horror at the news of the confirmed double scandal. Edmund is ill and miserable with grief and worry, but comforted by seeing Fanny. Their journey to Mansfield Park with Susan is a silent one, but Fanny is greeted with real enthusiasm by Lady Bertram.

> This eventful chapter shows Fanny, always something of an outsider amongst the Bertrams, and very much isolated from events in Portsmouth, at last returning to Mansfield Park to take up a central position in the family.

> The usually lazy Lady Bertram for once rushes to meet Fanny with 'no indolent step'; Lady Bertram's delight is motivated by a selfish desire to be comfortable, but the welcome is warm, nevertheless.

etourderie (French: *étourderie*) absent-mindedness

CHAPTER 47 (VOLUME III, CHAPTER xvi)

Unhappiness at Mansfield Park

The returning party finds Tom (still sick), Lady Bertram and Mrs Norris all in a very wretched state. Fanny learns the details of the events involving Maria and Julia from Lady Bertram. Mrs Norris is stupefied by the disastrous ending to the Rushworth marriage which she has prided herself upon arranging for her favourite niece, Maria. Her unfamiliar inertia means that she is not as spiteful to the newcomer, Susan, as she might have been if in full vigour. Susan is left much to herself and is able to make herself familiar with her new surroundings. Lady Bertram welcomes her and makes clear her genuine need of Fanny's presence.

After some time, Edmund is able to talk to Fanny about his full awakening to the shallow and even vicious nature of Mary Crawford.

She, he tells Fanny, felt the behaviour of her brother and Maria to have been indiscreet rather than abhorrent and behaved in an improperly flirtatious way after Edmund had chided her. Edmund accepts, finally, that her beauty and vivacity have deluded him about the depth of her cynicism. He is relieved to know that Fanny's affections have not become attached to Henry Crawford, in spite of his persistence.

> Fanny is shown as the strong character in the dismal aftermath of the disgrace of Maria and Julia. She is a thoughtful companion to Lady Bertram and the dear confidante of Edmund, who pours out his heart to her about his doomed love for Mary Crawford.

CHAPTER 48 (VOLUME III, CHAPTER xvii)

Epilogue; Fanny and Edmund are married

In spite of the dejection of those around her, Fanny is happy; she is needed and loved at Mansfield Park and has the deepest respect of Sir Thomas. Henry Crawford no longer pursues her and, best of all, Edmund is free of Mary.

Sir Thomas bitterly regrets the inadequacies of his children's upbringing; he finds his usual comfort in Edmund and is able to welcome an improvement in Tom's health and steadiness. He recognises only too well what a bad influence Mrs Norris has been and dismisses her suggestion that Maria – who is soon separated from Henry Crawford – should come back to Mansfield to live. Mrs Norris decides to leave and live as companion to the unfortunate Maria, at some distance from Mansfield Park: she is missed by no one. Julia and Yates are at least married and can be received; Henry Crawford is left to regret the loss of Fanny, who he might eventually have won. Relations between the Bertrams and the Grants are difficult after the behaviour of Mrs Grant's brother; conveniently, Dr Grant soon becomes a canon at Westminster Abbey and they leave Mansfield. Mary continues to live with her half-sister after his death (from over-indulgence at the dinner table), unable to find a husband who could equal Edmund.

Edmund himself recovers from his love for Mary rather sooner than he would have expected and realises that his ideal woman is very near to him. There are no hindrances to his marriage to Fanny; Sir Thomas has already begun to hope for the match and Lady Bertram, although reluctant to part with Fanny, is happy to have Susan as a substitute companion. Settled first in Edmund's parish at Thornton Lacey, they are able, on Dr Grant's death, to move back to the Parsonage at Mansfield Park, to general delight.

> In this final chapter the narrator draws attention to the duty of the author to 'restore every body, not greatly in fault themselves, to tolerable comfort, and to have done with all the rest': many futures are outlined.

> Many changes have taken place during the course of the narrative; the most central is Fanny's welcome as a wholly admirable daughter-in-law by Sir Thomas, who first took in the pathetic child with the decided view that she should never aspire to the same level in society as his own children. He reflects upon the virtues of the Price children he knows: Fanny, who they have all come to love dearly; William, with his 'continued good conduct, and rising fame'; and Susan, soon indispensable at Mansfield Park. He acknowledges 'the advantages of early hardship and discipline, and the consciousness of being born to struggle and endure'.

in another country in a different area, at some distance (as distinct from modern-day usage, which would mean 'outside England')

PART THREE

CRITICAL APPROACHES

CHARACTERISATION

The characters in the narrative offer perhaps the readiest means of beginning a critical approach to the novel as a whole. Jane Austen leaves a fair amount unwritten about her characters, so there is a temptation, which need not necessarily be avoided, for the reader to amplify certain aspects. Physical descriptions are scanty, while a politeness common to most of those who fill her pages sometimes disguises intention – the reader may work quite hard to supply some of the more superficial characteristics of Austen's cast. It is essential, however, in making a study of her characters, to examine carefully what they say to and about each other, and what the narrator has to say about their thoughts and reactions: this is the crucial evidence on which to base an analysis.

SIR THOMAS BERTRAM

Sir Thomas Bertram is not an aristocrat, but a member of the solid upper-middle class, with no family history recorded in the novel. His baronetcy may be a new one. As the owner of well-ordered Mansfield Park, he is apparently all that is dignified, responsible and principled. Yet much of the novel's darker side has its source in his character. He dutifully takes his seat in Parliament and runs his estates in England and Antigua with personal attention (see Political Background and Recent Criticism on the slave trade); he has given thought to his children's education; he is charitable to the Prices. And yet he has married a foolish and self-centred woman; unapproachable and stern himself, he has allowed his unsuitable sister-in-law to have too much influence with his children. The education he has offered them has been directed at social accomplishments and lacks a moral foundation. As a result, his elder son is a selfish wastrel and his daughters disgrace him. His growing appreciation of the sound qualities of the niece to whom he has given a home do not extend to a respect for her refusal to marry Henry Crawford, for whom she has neither love nor trust.

At the end of the narrative, Sir Thomas recognises what has been wrong in his role as a father:

> Wretchedly did he feel, that with all the cost and care of an anxious and expensive education, he had brought up his daughters without their understanding their first duties, or his being acquainted with their character and temper. (p. 382)

He is closely associated with Mansfield Park itself, which is for his niece the ideal home, but for his heir a property to be exploited, and for his daughters somewhere from which to escape. Looking with approval at Fanny and William, he has to acknowledge privately the advantages in character formation of hardship in upbringing – something which a landowner in his position would, though, not wish to see his own children endure, however beneficial the outcome. Sir Thomas perhaps suffers the severest self-examination of all the characters and comes to a genuine degree of self-knowledge in the end.

LADY BERTRAM

Suffering from 'a little ill-health, and a great deal of indolence' (p. 18), Sir Thomas's wife is without malice, but somewhat lazy and self-centred. She graces her establishment but can hardly be said to take charge of it. Her beauty has secured her a wealthier marriage than she might have expected with 'only seven thousand pounds' of her own (p. 5). She has acquitted herself well as the producer of an heir and three other children and rests on her laurels. Slow-witted (she does not grasp the rules of Speculation and is a card-table partner to be dreaded) and seldom aroused to any display of emotion, she is a complaisant figure at Mansfield Park. She allows herself to be guided into correct feelings by her husband, but 'Her affections were not acute, nor was her mind tenacious' (p. 371). She is fond of her husband, but oblivious to the dangers of his journey abroad. Her faint pleasure at seeing him home again is manifested by her moving her pet dog, for once, to make room for Sir Thomas on her sofa.

TOM BERTRAM

Sir Thomas's heir is a lively but heedless young man, about whose friends and activities his father is anxious. He runs through money carelessly, endangering in the process his brother's future livelihood. He seems to undertake no useful duties on the Mansfield estates, although he takes advantage of the opportunity to shoot game there with friends. He is very personable, easily persuading most of the Mansfield entourage into undertaking amateur dramatics, and his drive – with that of his friend Yates – carries the production through almost to performance. Tom takes life lightly: in spite of his knowledge that his father would not under any circumstances approve of the theatricals, he feels genuine enjoyment at the ludicrous confrontation 'on stage' between the 'ranting' Yates and his astounded father.

After his illness at the end of the narrative, he reproaches himself and becomes, perhaps not altogether convincingly, 'useful to his father, steady and quiet, and not living merely for himself' (p. 381).

Edmund bertram

Edmund is the younger son of Sir Thomas; destined for the clergy, his ordination takes place during the course of the narrative. A high-minded and earnest young man, he takes his vocation seriously, unlike some clergymen of his day. He is the one member of the family who befriends the unhappy Fanny in her early days at Mansfield Park. He recognises her intelligence and a seriousness to match his own and becomes her adviser and teacher.

Edmund is made utterly miserable by his infatuation with Mary Crawford, who plays with his affections. On the one hand she is angry that he will not give up his vocation, and on the other is attracted by his good looks: one of her London friends, she reports, 'declares she knows but three men in town who have so good a person, height, and air' (p. 344). Finally acknowledging the irretrievable shallowness of Mary Crawford's character, Edmund turns to his cousin and confidante for comfort in his misery, reversing the nature of their earlier relationship.

Sooner than expected, he realises that his ideal wife is nearer at hand than he had imagined, and he settles into domestic happiness with Fanny. Edmund has often been seen by readers as a somewhat dull hero: his high-mindedness can be seen as contrasting (to Edmund's disadvantage) with Henry Crawford's charm and entertaining style (see Critical History and Broader Perspectives).

MARIA BERTRAM

Sir Thomas's elder daughter is handsome and confident and has been brought up by her father to take her place in society. Sir Thomas has been too rigorous, Lady Bertram has been too vague, and Mrs Norris has flattered the girls and offered no principles at all. Maria and her sister do nothing to make Fanny feel at home in her early days at Mansfield and are generally wilful and spoilt.

During Sir Thomas's lengthy absence, Maria seizes the opportunity to indulge in a flirtation with Henry Crawford, in spite of her informal engagement to the foolish but wealthy Mr Rushworth. Even when married, she retains her strong attachment to Henry and, apparently almost on a whim, she runs away with him – a socially unforgiveable act at the time of the narrative. Once the adulterous relationship has ended, she suffers the horrible fate of having to share a home with her Aunt Norris. Proud and headstrong as she is, Maria is nevertheless easy prey to Henry Crawford, a practised seducer.

JULIA BERTRAM

Julia is the younger, equally handsome and confident Bertram daughter. She, too, easily falls victim to the charm of Henry Crawford, and his preference for her sister leads to a coolness between them. However, the sisters become close again on Maria's marriage, and Julia becomes her sister's constant companion, not returning to Mansfield Park even when there is great distress at home over Tom's serious illness.

Julia's liking for the glamorous life of Brighton and London, and her lack of moral principles, again echo her sister's characteristics. Her fear of a loss of freedom following Maria's adulterous flight seems to be what prompts her elopement with Yates. Her 'crime' is less serious than her sister's, since she and Yates are married; they are forgiven, and can be accepted into society again.

FANNY PRICE

The narrative of *Mansfield Park* deals centrally with the development of Fanny, whose mother describes her as 'a very well-disposed, good-humoured girl … somewhat delicate and puny' (p. 11). She matures from a timid, anxious and little-noticed girl to become a composed young woman able to respond to the needs of others and well able to take her place in society with the husband she has wanted from early years. Overlooked, teased by her girl cousins and treated maliciously by Mrs Norris, Fanny is unhappy and homesick during her first months at Mansfield – 'sobbing herself to sleep' although showing only a 'quiet, passive manner' (p. 14) to the Bertrams. She finds a friend and mentor in her cousin Edmund, who quickly appreciates her qualities and guides her development and education. She has no desire to acquire the polite accomplishments of her cousins – a little watercolour painting and music – but is a dedicated reader. After the governess leaves, the old schoolroom – now the East room – becomes Fanny's own refuge.

Fanny shares Edmund's principled views – he is to become a clergyman – and soon falls in love with him. She has to suffer a lengthy period of anguish as an observer of his infatuation with the alluring Mary Crawford. She suffers greatly, too, when Henry Crawford courts her against her will, and particularly when – because of her rejection of such an excellent offer – she deeply offends her uncle, who had earlier begun to appreciate his niece. Fanny endures a different kind of suffering when Sir Thomas shrewdly sends her on a visit 'home' to Portsmouth. As he expected, the dirt and disorder of her parents' house is very distressing to her, and she realises that her true home is at Mansfield Park. It becomes clear, as disasters multiply for the Bertrams, that she is really needed there.

Of course, the witty, vivacious and sophisticated Mary Crawford offers a strong contrast to Fanny, and some readers (see Critical History and Broader Perspectives) have found her a heroine lacking in attractive qualities. She tends to be described in terms such as 'modest', 'shy', 'pretty', with a 'sweet temper' and a 'grateful heart'. But by the end of the novel, her position is secure: 'she was useful, she was beloved' and had the 'perfect approbation and increased regard' of Sir Thomas (p. 380). She is a little dull, maybe, yet the qualities that have brought the nervous child through to social success and a happy marriage should not be underrated: she is perceptive as well as observant; she is quite tough-minded and will not move from her considered position (about theatricals, when even

Edmund weakened, or about Henry's courtship); she is resilient and persevering in her patient loyalty to Edmund.

MRS NORRIS

Fanny's Aunt Norris lives nearby at the White House after being widowed. She is one of Jane Austen's most memorable monsters; the source of much comedy for the reader, she is nevertheless a malign figure in the narrative. Always motivated by self-interest, she is a sycophantic hanger-on at Mansfield Park. Claiming to be indispensable, she is in fact a determined meddler who interferes to everyone's detriment. Many minor examples of her interference occur and cause much of the humour associated with her outrageous character – as described before Fanny's ball, for instance, when she is 'entirely taken up at first in fresh arranging and injuring the noble fire which the butler had prepared' (pp. 225–6). Real damage is done by her, too, in spoiling and pandering to the young Bertrams, and particularly by her promotion of the disastrous marriage of her favourite, Maria, and the feeble-minded and unsuitable Mr Rushworth.

To Fanny, who – as Mrs Norris frequently reminds her – is of lower social standing, she is really spiteful, never losing an opportunity to belittle her and demanding endless attention and errands from Fanny.

DR & MRS GRANT

Mrs Grant is a kindly and good-natured woman, who lives at Mansfield Parsonage with her husband, the bad-tempered and fussy Dr Grant – fifteen years her senior. She manages the awkwardness of their marriage by giving way to his whims, but her own even temperament is preserved. Although her half-sister, Mary Crawford, describes Mrs Grant as the 'perfect wife', the reader recognises that this is a far from perfect marriage, and the unpleasant aspects of Dr Grant's character may well go some way to reinforcing Mary's distaste for clergymen. With a greedy husband (it is Dr Grant's appetite that kills him off in Chapter 48), Mrs Grant is a lavish provider of food, much to the disgust of Mrs Norris, who believes that not only the quantity of food but even the generous size of her dining table is inappropriate to her social standing.

MARY CRAWFORD

Mary's beauty, sophistication and London style make her a sparkling figure at the usually sober Mansfield Park, where she is welcomed for her personal charm and witty conversation. But she is a worldly creature: attracted to Edmund, she is prepared to overlook his clerical vocation as a bar to marriage only when it seems that his elder brother is likely to die, leaving him as heir to Sir Thomas.

Professing herself a friend of Fanny's and, indeed, well aware of Fanny's real qualities, she nevertheless participates with relish – as if playing a game – in her brother's courtship plans. 'Complaisant as a sister', she is 'careless as a woman and a friend' (p. 215). Her fundamental lack of principle becomes clear to Fanny, who sees 'a mind led astray and bewildered, and without any suspicion of being so; darkened, yet fancying itself light' (p. 304). Edmund is slower to admit Mary's grave faults, only finally recognising them when Mary's reaction to the shame of her brother's elopement with Maria shows that she regrets the discovery rather than the deed. A wealthy young woman, Mary is left unmarried and regretting the loss of Edmund in the glance into the future offered at the end of the novel.

HENRY CRAWFORD

Henry is 'not handsome', but has 'air and countenance' (p. 36), and shares with his sister the 'popular manners' which make them socially sought after. His talents in acting and reading aloud are unquestioned and, in fact, he is continually playing a part, or imagining a role, throughout the narrative. Even Fanny, who sensibly mistrusts him from the start, is moved by his reading from Shakespeare, although he claims to know nothing of the text he has just read.

He enjoys testing his powers of seduction, and plays with the affections of both Julia and Maria – in the case of the latter, challenged by her engagement to Rushworth. Fanny's indifference is seen by him as an even greater provocation, perhaps, and he takes on the role of the constant lover with what might be the beginnings of success, before he suddenly and rashly elopes with the married but still besotted Maria. There is evidence of his sexual allure beyond the unsophisticated tastes of

Mansfield: his sister admires Fanny for capturing the heart of her brother 'who has been shot at by so many' (p. 300).

His character is mercurial; he imagines himself playing the part of a clergyman when talking to Edmund, and that of a sailor when with William. Usually a lax landowner, when talking to Fanny he imagines himself taking on the duties he has neglected. His charm is manifest; he is nevertheless corrupt and, like his sister, a destructive force in the narrative.

JOHN YATES

The Hon. John Yates is introduced as Tom's friend, a visitor to Mansfield Park. As Julia is something of a shadow to her sister, Maria, so Yates, the younger son of an earl, is cast in rather the same mould as Henry Crawford. A member of a fast group in London society, and addicted to the theatre, he is neither as good an actor as Crawford, nor as corrupt in his relationships with women. Julia and Yates escape the wretchedness that ends the ill-judged runaway romance of Maria and Henry Crawford, and in fact the repentant pair seem able to look forward to a reasonably contented future.

Like the Crawfords, Yates is a destabilising influence at Mansfield. He is an aristocrat and therefore viewed with suspicion by Sir Thomas, who is of the respectable upper-middle class. It is in keeping with what Sir Thomas sees as the loose morals of Yates's class that he should introduce the idea of a production of *Lovers' Vows* at Mansfield Park, having come from a theatrical party at an aristocratic house (see Social Background on amateur theatricals).

MRS RUSHWORTH

At Sotherton, Mrs Rushworth is the widow of the head of an even wealthier and probably more established family than that of Sir Thomas Bertram. She is the chatelaine of an ancient Elizabethan house, around which she is proud to escort the Bertram party. She is devoted to her foolish son and happy to welcome Maria as her daughter-in-law, behaving with discretion and tact by leaving for Bath on their marriage. Although described as 'well-meaning', she is a somewhat comic figure who fusses and takes too long to show her visitors over the house, about which she has learned the history parrot-fashion. Nevertheless, she has to be taken seriously when matrimonial disaster looms. Her position in society is unassailable, and her outrage at Maria's shameful treatment of her son represents the general disapproval of a society which will not forgive such behaviour.

MR RUSHWORTH

Mr Rushworth is disgracefully treated by his wife (Maria) and Henry Crawford, but his vanity and foolishness mean that little sympathy is felt for him. Accepted as a desirable suitor for Maria, at first only Edmund finds James Rushworth lacking, believing 'If this man had not twelve thousand a year, he would be a very stupid fellow' (p. 35). Rushworth takes a childish delight in dressing up for the theatricals at Mansfield Park, and is memorable for his excitement about his pink satin cloak, although he has to have his speeches cut to a minimum as his memory is not equal to the task of much learning. Sir Thomas can see that he is an unsuitable husband for his daughter but, against his better judgement, allows the ill-fated marriage to go ahead. In the final chapter, the narrator imagines that the disappointed, disgruntled and divorced Rushworth may be lured by a pretty face into a second marriage – and may this time be fortunate enough to find a better-natured partner.

MR PRICE

At Portsmouth, Fanny's father is a source of disappointment and even shame to her; on their first meeting for many years, she is 'sadly pained by his language and his smell of spirits' (p. 315). A retired naval lieutenant, his world in Portsmouth is very limited, centring almost entirely on naval matters. Unimaginative and insensitive, he is hardly aware of his daughter's presence in the house. Although usually coarse and unrefined, he can on occasion be socially adroit, as when he meets Henry Crawford, whose attentions to Fanny make her a little more interesting in Mr Price's eyes.

MRS PRICE

Mrs Price is even more disappointing to Fanny than her father is. Fanny hopes for the development of a strong relationship with her mother, but this does not happen. It is not surprising to the reader, since poor Mrs Price (who has given birth to nine children), lives on the brink of domestic disaster: her younger children are out of control; her household is dirty, noisy and disorganised; and her servants are lazy and disobedient. Even the loyal William says that the house is 'always in confusion' (p. 308) and he hopes that Fanny, during her visit, may be able to help bring some order – a task which seems to be beyond what is possible. Fanny's assessment of her mother is harsh, as 'a partial, ill-judging parent, a dawdle, a slattern, who neither taught nor restrained her children, whose house was the scene of mismanagement and discomfort … and who had no talent, no conversation, no affection towards herself' (p. 324).

She is always muddled and hard-pressed, yet in her Sunday best Mrs Price is as 'handsome' as her sister, Lady Bertram; she lacks the energy, however, of her other sister, Mrs Norris, which the narrator points out would have stood her in good stead, with so much to do. It is suggested that, had she not made an unwise marriage to the unsuccessful Lieutenant Price, she could perhaps have led a more comfortable life. Mrs Price offers an awful warning, in the context of the narrative's commentary on marriage, of the folly of marrying without consideration of financial matters. Paradoxically, against this must be set the fact that it is the Price children, brought up in unsatisfactory circumstances, who provide the sterling characters amongst the young in the novel.

WILLIAM PRICE

William is a personable young man, beloved elder brother of Fanny, and a dedicated sailor (see Jane Austen's Life on Austen's naval brothers). He is warm-hearted, attached to his family and particularly to Fanny. His sound principles combined with a zest for life make him an attractive character – perhaps the most attractive in the novel. Helped financially by his uncle, Sir Thomas Bertram, he acquits himself well as a young midshipman; his uncle listens approvingly as he gives an account of the dangers and adventures of the seven years he has spent at sea. In his account may be seen 'the proof of good principles, professional knowledge, energy, courage, and cheerfulness—every thing that could deserve or promise well' (p. 196). However, his story offers an example of one of Jane Austen's recurrent themes: the significance in life of wealth and influence. He fears that, even with Sir Thomas's support, without appropriate influence he is unlikely to gain promotion in the navy. Henry Crawford, with his own interests in mind, persuades his disreputable uncle, the retired admiral, to use his position to forward William's ambitions, which he successfully does. The final chapter refers briefly to William and his 'continued good conduct, and rising fame' (p. 389).

SUSAN PRICE

At Portsmouth Fanny soon recognises her younger sister's strength of character and realises that her displays of temper are the result of her struggles to bring some order to the chaos which exists in the Price household. Susan is only too happy to escape from Portsmouth with her sister. Physically and mentally more robust than Fanny at the same age, Susan copes well with the difficulties associated with her arrival at a time of grief and anxiety for all. With her 'more fearless disposition and happier nerves' (p. 389), Susan is able to make herself at home at Mansfield Park and eventually take Fanny's place as companion to her aunt, Lady Bertram, when her sister and Edmund marry.

SETTINGS

MANSFIELD PARK

Houses are often central to Jane Austen's novels, both as fascinating in themselves and, particularly, as representing solid evidence of wealth and status. (Readers of *Pride and Prejudice* will recollect the awed delight of Elizabeth Bennet on seeing Pemberley House, the home of Mr Darcy, for the first time: 'at that moment she felt, that to be mistress of Pemberley might be something!') Mansfield Park is Austen's prime example, the house giving its name to the novel and mentioned in both the first and the last sentences of the narrative. Most significantly, the reader is bound to see the grand house as contributing to the unease which much of the novel creates: apparently the orderly setting for all that is virtuous in English country life, it is also home to characters ranging from the idle to the dissolute. Of the Mansfield Park entourage, Lady Bertram is 'indolent', Mrs Norris is malicious to the point of being vicious, Maria and Julia are at the very least wilful and rash over their liaisons, Tom is selfish and dissipated, and Sir Thomas himself displays moral ambivalence (see Characterisation).

Unlike Sotherton, Mansfield Park is not methodically described. When Fanny Price arrives as a child, she is amazed at the 'grandeur' of the house: the rooms seem 'too large for her to move in with ease' (p. 14). We do have a good description (pp. 125–7) of the East room, once the schoolroom and soon Fanny's own refuge; the humble trappings of her fireless sitting room – an addition to her tiny attic bedroom – serve to point out her inferior position in the household, as well as to illustrate her interests. The drawing room, the dining room and the breakfast room are all mentioned as the family moves about the daily round; during the course of the narrative, the billiard room becomes the theatre, Sir Thomas's room the green room (the actors' preparation room); and we know there is a ballroom. We also know, for instance, that there are sofas in the drawing room and at least one bookcase in Sir Thomas's room, but the style of the house remains elusive. It is a 'modern built house' and it is implied from the comments about Sotherton that Mansfield Park itself is furnished in a modern fashion. The grounds feature a shrubbery – a relatively new feature at that time. If Sir Thomas is the descendant of a long line of country gentry, we are told nothing about it. The house, run by an army of servants and estate workers, exists only in the present; so far as the narrative goes, it has no past.

Orderly, spacious and comfortable, Mansfield Park – at first fearsome to Fanny – becomes all that is perfect to her: when she is at Portsmouth she realises 'Mansfield was home'. That she finally settles as Mrs Bertram at the Parsonage 'within the view and patronage of Mansfield Park' (p. 390) can be interpreted in more ways than one (see Recent Criticism).

SOTHERTON

The seat of the Rushworths, Sotherton is an Elizabethan house with extensive grounds and estate. The Rushworth family is wealthier than Sir Thomas's and possibly longer established. The house is contrasted with Mansfield Park and its implied modern amenities; it is amply furnished in the taste of 'fifty years back', there are more rooms than use could easily be found for and, in Mr Rushworth's view, the whole establishment is ripe for 'improvement'. Tradition in this ancient house is already weakened, as shown, for instance, in the visit to the chapel, where daily prayers for family and servants have been abandoned, and also in the discussion about the ancient oak avenue, which represents landscape design of a much earlier time and is destined to be felled.

Mr Rushworth intends to employ Humphry Repton, the leading landscape gardener and successor to 'Capability' Brown, who belonged to what was known as the 'Naturalist' school of the eighteenth century and reacted to the more formally structured layouts – such as the avenue of oaks – previously admired. Straight lines and level areas were abhorrent to the Naturalists: curved paths, undulating grassy areas and irregularly shaped lakes were desirable. It seems that Sotherton has previously received the attentions of a Naturalist designer, since it already has a wilderness, a woodland area and a park edged by a ha-ha, which was a ditch division adapted by 'Capability' Brown from a French design to keep deer or cattle away, without the interruption a fence would make to the sweep of the grass. Repton is obviously expected to introduce the even newer 'Picturesque' features popular at the beginning of the nineteenth century, such as artificially devised waterfalls, hillocks and the importation of craggy rocks. Such 'improvements' would have been the subject of much discussion in Jane Austen's day, and there is a division in *Mansfield Park* between the modernisers and those who respect the oak avenue.

Generally, Sotherton can be seen as representing a long-established gentry, which has lost much of its respect for tradition, yet failed to understand modern life. (See Language and Style on the use of the grounds in forwarding romantic attachments during the visit to Sotherton.)

PORTSMOUTH

In the Price household, Jane Austen portrays a family who are hanging on grimly to the fringes of gentility, but in circumstances more squalid than those she describes anywhere else.

Fanny is wretched there, naturally. The family warmth she believed she remembered and hoped to renew does not materialise; the house is small and inconvenient and its inhabitants are insensitive and lack civilised manners. But there is high comedy, too, in the account of the dirty, noisy, badly managed household. Meals never arrive on time and are marked by unappetising cooking and filthy crockery and cutlery. The servants are out of Mrs Price's control and, living cheek by jowl as they do with the family, there is a little rounding out of their characters: Rebecca, 'a trollopy-looking maid-servant' (p. 312), gets away with being lazy, incompetent and rebellious; the reader could contrast her with the skilful, unobtrusive and extensive staff at Mansfield Park, or with the two maids who were dismissed at Sotherton for wearing white dresses. Mrs Price fears that, on her Sunday walk to the naval chapel, she might suffer the indignity of seeing her servant 'pass by with a flower in her hat' (p. 338), which would apparently be several degrees worse than discovering servant girls in white dresses.

Portsmouth itself is seen as unsuitable for Fanny. Although she enjoys the opportunity of a walk in the fresh air after the frowstiness of the house, sea air is seen by the Crawfords as detrimental to a young lady's health and complexion.

As Sir Thomas had intended, Fanny appreciates the comfort, order and calm of Mansfield Park more than ever; he expects her, as a result of her experience of straitened circumstances, to accept Crawford's offer of marriage and the position in society which his wealth would bring.

LONDON

In *Mansfield Park*, London represents the sophisticated but dangerous pleasures of theatres, parties and amorous liaisons. Although the principled Sir Thomas spends time in London related to his parliamentary duties, the city's moral tone is represented as decidedly dubious. The reprobate admiral, the Crawfords' uncle, lives there; Henry and Mary Crawford are socially at home there; Maria and Julia – once they are swallowed up by its delights – are unwilling to return to Mansfield Park. Young people like the Crawfords, caught up in London's social whirl, are seen as morally tainted: amusing and wealthy, but engaged entirely in the pursuit of pleasure; and cultivated, but unprincipled.

Jane Austen is known for her avoidance of political comment or mention of wider issues of the day. However, it is worth bearing in mind that, in 1811, when the author began *Mansfield Park*, the dissolute Prince of Wales was finally appointed Regent, after his father, King George III, declined yet again into mental instability. The Prince Regent's extravagant displays in London and his scandalous private life made the head of state a notorious figure, and fashionable London was thought a morally dangerous place by the respectable. Fanny never goes to London during the course of the narrative; she 'was disposed to think the influence of London very much at war with all respectable attachments' (p. 357) and certainly it is the setting particularly for sexual misbehaviour in the novel, as well as contrasting in moral tone with the country, as represented by Mansfield Park and Sotherton.

NARRATIVE MODES

Jane Austen presents an **omniscient narrator**, that is, a narrator who is able to describe the thoughts as well as the actions of the characters. Generally, the narrator is engaged in forwarding the events which make up the story, but occasionally offers some direct commentary to the reader, as in the opening paragraph of *Mansfield Park*: 'But there certainly are not so many men of large fortune in the world, as there are pretty women to deserve them' (p. 5). The narrator's relationship with the reader is a comfortable one, inviting enjoyment of the tale to be unfolded, of course, as well as making assumptions about the reader's complicity with the **tone**.

Should we identify the narrator with Jane Austen herself? Critics of narrative style argue over this point, and certainly it cannot be taken for granted that author and narrator are one. However, Jane Austen does tempt the reader to this view in her final chapter when the now intrusive narrator reminds us of an authorial presence, in describing the central character as 'My Fanny', hinting, for once, at subjective involvement. The narrator goes on to outline, in the first person, the novelist's need to round off the story and, at the end of the final chapter, invites the reader to set appropriate dates for Edmund's falling in love with Fanny: 'I purposely abstain from dates on this occasion, that every one may be at liberty to fix their own' (p. 387). Many readers like to believe that, particularly at the opening and closing of her novel, Jane Austen's own voice is evident; others, that the narrator is, as it were, another character in the novel's structure.

The narrator uses often quite formal description, as for instance in the introduction of each member of the cast of players, usually by means of a brief account of his or her status, characteristics and, sometimes, appearance. But much of *Mansfield Park* consists of the thoughts of the characters and, of course, dialogue or conversation, which excludes the narrative **voice**. The earnest, intimate chats between Fanny and Edmund are very revealing of their natures; and, equally, the vivacious private conversations between the Crawford brother and sister gradually expose the depth of their cynicism. Jane Austen is a skilled handler of the group conversation, too – as in the evening at the Parsonage (Chapter 25), for example, when card games are played and the plot and character developments are forwarded on several fronts.

Jane Austen was one of the first English novelists to use a narrative device usually known as **free indirect speech** or **discourse**, which fuses the voices of narrator and character. Fanny's train of thought is offered by these means after the ball when her brother has departed early (p. 233), or at length in the paragraph (after she has received a letter from Mary Crawford) beginning, 'This was a letter to be run through eagerly' (p. 344).

The narrative in Volume III of Fanny's exile in Portsmouth owes something to the **epistolary novel**, a story told in exchanges of correspondence. Austen had experimented with this form in an early version of *Sense and Sensibility*. With Fanny isolated from the rest of the characters, the events which forward the narrative are conveyed by letters from Edmund, Mary Crawford and Lady Bertram. However, the author avoids the limitations of this device by incorporating the correspondence into the broad range of narrative modes she has at her command.

It is usually assumed, from various clues in the novel, that the main events of *Mansfield Park* take place at about the time Jane Austen was writing: that is, roughly between 1811 and 1813–14. The reference (p. 130) to *Crabbe's Tales*, published in September 1812, is often taken as an indication of the time scale, although Austen probably mentioned the volume in order to demonstrate Fanny's modern tastes. The exact dates are not necessarily important: what is relevant is that it was a contemporary and topical novel of its day.

The chronological length of *Mansfield Park* exceeds the tight time scheme of Jane Austen's other novels, which is usually between six months and a year. There is a lengthy introduction to the main events, going back thirty years to the marriages of the three Ward sisters, and describing the later 'adoption' of Fanny into the Bertram family and her early unhappiness. However, with the arrival of the Crawfords at Mansfield in the July after Fanny turns eighteen, the main events of the novel begin. The narrative ends, but for a projection into the future lives of the characters, early in the following summer.

During this period of less than a year, events take place in a chronologically straightforward way, until Fanny goes away to Portsmouth. In an essay on aspects of Jane Austen's work in *After Bakhtin* (1990), David Lodge writes about the reader's experience of time in different genres of fiction: the tempo of a thriller, for instance, can seem faster than reality, that of a **stream of consciousness** novel slower. But Jane Austen's novels, he writes, 'seem to have the tempo of life itself, yet their stories occupy several months, and the reading of them takes only a few hours' (p. 125). Lodge attributes Jane Austen's success in creating something that seems like 'real' time largely to her presentation of events in a series of scenes, in which conversation dominates. He describes conversation as 'neutral' in narrative time, since reading it takes about the same time as hearing it would.

The chronological evenness of the narrative is dislocated jarringly when Fanny is cut off from the other characters in Portsmouth; there is also dislocation of time (as well as place) in Sir Thomas's absence abroad (see comment on geographical dislocation by Edward Said in Recent Criticism). Sir Thomas moves into a time sphere which is separated from that of Mansfield by the passage of time which must elapse between sending and receiving correspondence. Even upon receipt of a letter, those at Mansfield have no certain knowledge as to whether he is still alive or dead, well or ill, successful or unsuccessful in his enterprise. This dislocation of time is adjusted with something of a thunderclap when Sir Thomas re-enters Mansfield time and stops the rehearsal at the climax of Volume I.

Fanny's isolation at her natural home (Portsmouth) is rendered even more pitiful in much the same way: she suffers dislocation of place and of time, since she is constantly anxious about events at Mansfield and in London. Any news she gets is a day or two old – that is, already in the past – and she (and probably the reader) dreads what might be happening in the present. Unlike Sir Thomas's re-entry into the central time and place of the novel, restoring his house to material order, Fanny's return to Mansfield Park heralds a spiritual renewal.

STRUCTURE

Both the narrative modes and the time pattern (see above) help to establish the structure of a novel. The demands of the plot and the realisation of themes are also key elements. In the case of *Mansfield Park*, the plot structure is that required by the heroine-centred love story or **sentimental novel**, of which Richardson's *Pamela, or Virtue Rewarded* (1740) is a classic example. This genre requires a happy ending in which the heroine marries the man she loves after experiencing an extended sequence of difficulties. It is usual for the heroine in Jane Austen's novels to wait patiently and, as a rule, passively for the realisation of her dreams. In Fanny's case, she has to endure seeing her adored Edmund fall in love with and court another woman, before he eventually realises the worthlessness of Mary and the virtues of Fanny. She also suffers the unwanted attentions of a rake and, earlier, the indignities of being brought up as a poor relation, which made it difficult for her to take her place in Mansfield society.

It is the obstacles in the way of the heroine's fulfilment that create the tension in the structure. The **peripeteia** (the sudden change of fortunes represented by the abrupt flight of Maria and Henry Crawford) breaks the tension, proving Fanny right in her rejection of Henry, and leading to Edmund's rejection of Henry Crawford's unprincipled sister.

The long tradition of narrative **realism** was in its early stages at the time Jane Austen was writing, but she developed it to a high degree within the constraints she set herself. The main factor limiting her scope is her preference for the familiar. She wrote to her niece, Anna Austen, who wanted to become a novelist, '3 or 4 families in a Country Village is the very thing to work on' (1814). Writing in 1816 to her nephew, James-Edward Austen-Leigh, she described her famous view of her own work: 'the little bit (two Inches wide) of Ivory, on which I work with so fine a brush, as produces little effect after much labour.' In spite of this clear description of her set purpose, as a kind of miniaturist, she has been often criticised for leaving out so much – wars, politics, social problems and sex, for instance.

That Jane Austen is so widely read nearly two hundred years after her work first appeared is indicative, however, of the value of her work, and perhaps what is always admired is the elegance and wit of her narratives. The harmony of the style of the whole by no means limits its variety, and the defining elements of Austen's style can be seen to be the range of narrative techniques described above. The **authorial voice**, or the **omniscient narrator**'s voice, demands a formal and almost judicial style, which can be censorious in *Mansfield Park* in relation to the characters' shortcomings, but is usually well leavened with humour and **irony**. **Free indirect speech** and narrative with a character-based viewpoint show a marked shift in style to a lighter **tone**, which usually has the effect of increasing the pace of the novel. **Direct speech**, of which there is a great deal in the form of various conversations, offers the opportunity of character development and requires appropriate speech patterns – Tom, for instance, speaks in a colloquial style (the new incumbent is likely to 'pop off', he says) which contrasts with that of his father or the more sober Edmund. Mary Crawford's conversation is amusing and sometimes improper, whereas shy Fanny speaks little in public and her longer speeches sometimes show her apparently trying out some ideas from the books she has been reading. Mrs Norris's fussy, malicious or ingratiating speech goes a long way towards establishing her character.

Jane Austen's use of **direct speech** is generally deployed in a series of greater or lesser 'scenes' – an appropriate term, since they contain much dialogue, as in a play. She assembles her characters – two, three or more – usually indoors: in a drawing room, at the dinner table, around the fire, at an evening party, at rehearsal, at a ball. The stage-like effect is lost in the occasional outdoor scenes, as at Sotherton. Given her self-imposed constraints of writing from experience or observation, it is not surprising that she has few scenes in which men are alone together, although the uncomfortable but very funny meeting of Sir Thomas and Mr Yates, watched by Tom, is an exception.

There is surprisingly little of what could be called 'descriptive' writing in *Mansfield Park*. Items of food are sometimes identified, aspects of the countryside get a passing reference, but personal appearance and dress are only cursorily mentioned. Characters might be dark or fair, 'handsome' or not, while a dress might be becoming or not – little else is offered. In *Mansfield Park* the reader can find a scarlet face or two, a green curtain, some white dresses, a grey pony and an amber cross; but on the whole, colour is conspicuously absent from Jane Austen's novels. Such detail as she does give is accurate (she meticulously researched detail such as the existence of hedges in Northamptonshire, which she did not previously know, for instance). There is no doubt, though, that the reader has a good deal of work to do in supplying descriptive detail; it is worth remembering, of course, that she wrote for a social circle never less than genteel, or aspiring to gentility; her contemporary readers were well able to supply those details – about characters similar to themselves – of which we might feel a lack.

Equally, Jane Austen's first readers may well have known the play *Lovers' Vows*, which adds a dimension of **intertextuality** to the novel (see commentary to Chapter 14 in Detailed Summaries for a brief account of this play). There are not always direct parallels between the characters of the play and the roles adopted by the Mansfield party, but the themes of lovers' misfortunes, seduction and betrayal, and the radical **Romanticism** of the work are apt in the light of subsequent events. There are many literary references in *Mansfield Park*: Fanny's favourite reading not only shows Edmund's guidance but can also reveal much about her way of thinking. Again, her contemporary readers would have been familiar with much of what is mentioned, or at least know something about it; this is more difficult for modern readers and it could well be worthwhile for the Austen student to study a little of Fanny's reading matter. This includes writing by William Cowper, Walter Scott, Samuel

Johnson and George Crabbe. In Crabbe's *The Parish Register* (1807) a virtuous and steadfast character called Fanny Price figures – this is probably the source of the name for Jane Austen's heroine.

Shakespeare is mentioned several times in *Mansfield Park*, centrally in the case of Henry Crawford's mesmerising reading from *Henry VIII*. Readers familiar with *A Midsummer Night's Dream* will have noticed parallels between Shakespeare's lovers' tangles in the woods outside Athens and the pairings and games of hide and seek in the grounds of Sotherton. Maybe, too, there is a touch of Cordelia (*King Lear*) about Fanny – the youngest and least regarded by Sir Thomas of the three Mansfield girls, she is honest and sincere, and eventually becomes the 'real' daughter who delights him, in contrast to his own wayward daughters.

Symbolism is a literary device which came into its own later in the nineteenth century. Its use can be said to run counter to the aims of **realism**; when it can be identified in *Mansfield Park* it is not a heavy presence. The oak trees at Sotherton may be seen as representing tradition; the game of Speculation is played in something of a symbolic way, perhaps. The Shakespearean parallels with *A Midsummer Night's Dream* can also be read in this way, and certainly the amber cross and its chain serve a symbolic purpose in the novel. The cross is a gift to Fanny from her brother; a token which traditionally protects from evil, it is a religious object, but one which may properly be worn by a young woman at a ball (Jane Austen had herself been given a similar cross – of topaz – by Charles, one of her sailor brothers). The conniving Crawfords plan to trap Fanny into accepting a gold necklace on which to wear the cross – indirectly a gift from Henry, and an embarrassment to Fanny when she discovers this. Fortunately, it is too large and a plain gold chain thoughtfully offered by Edmund is substituted to bear the cross. Fanny wears the necklace, too, out of politeness, but – protected by the gifts of her brother and her cousin – she is saved from this manifestation of the Crawfords' cunning.

PART FOUR

TEXTUAL ANALYSIS

TEXT 1 (PAGES 5–6)

Jane Austen's novels operate within the framework of love, marriage and money – often, as the opening paragraph of *Mansfield Park* shows, money and property can be dominant. This prologue, set thirty years before the beginning of the story proper, gives an account of the marriages of the three Ward sisters, who become the Mrs Norris, the Lady Bertram and the Mrs Price of the later narrative.

> About thirty years ago, Miss Maria Ward, of Huntingdon, with only seven thousand pounds, had the good luck to captivate Sir Thomas Bertram, of Mansfield Park, in the county of Northampton, and to be thereby raised to the rank of baronet's lady, with all the comforts and consequences of an handsome house and large income. All Huntingdon exclaimed on the greatness of the match, and her uncle, the lawyer, himself, allowed her to be at least three thousand pounds short of any equitable claim to it. She had two sisters to be benefited by her elevation, and such of their acquaintance as thought Miss Ward and Miss Frances quite as handsome as Miss Maria, did not scruple to predict their marrying with almost equal advantage. But there certainly are not so many men of large fortune in the world, as there are pretty women to deserve them. Miss Ward, at the end of half a dozen years, found herself obliged to be attached to the Rev. Mr. Norris, a friend of her brother-in-law, with scarcely any private fortune, and Miss Frances fared yet worse. Miss Ward's match, indeed, when it came to the point, was not contemptible, Sir Thomas being happily able to give his friend an income in the living of Mansfield, and Mr. and Mrs. Norris began their career of conjugal felicity with very little less than a thousand a year. But Miss Frances married, in the common phrase, to disoblige her family, and by fixing on a Lieutenant of Marines, without education, fortune, or connections, did it very thoroughly. She could hardly have made a more untoward choice. Sir Thomas Bertram had interest, which, from principle as well as pride, from a general wish of doing right, and a desire of seeing all that were connected with him in situations of respectability, he would have been glad to exert for the advantage of Lady Bertram's sister; but her husband's profession was such as no interest could reach;

and before he had time to devise any other method of assisting them, an absolute breach between the sisters had taken place. It was the natural result of the conduct of each party, and such as a very imprudent marriage almost always produces. To save herself from useless remonstrance, Mrs. Price never wrote to her family on the subject till actually married. Lady Bertram, who was a woman of very tranquil feelings, and a temper remarkably easy and indolent, would have contented herself with merely giving up her sister, and thinking no more of the matter; but Mrs. Norris had a spirit of activity, which could not be satisfied till she had written a long and angry letter to Fanny, to point out the folly of her conduct, and threaten her with all its possible ill consequences. Mrs. Price in her turn was injured and angry; and an answer which comprehended each sister in its bitterness, and bestowed such very disrespectful reflections on the pride of Sir Thomas, as Mrs. Norris could not possibly keep to herself, put an end to all intercourse between them for a considerable period.

The alliance of the middle sister, Maria, with a baronet is ascribed to 'good luck', since she had only seven thousand pounds, apparently 'at least three thousand pounds short' of the going rate for the dowry of a girl who was to marry a baronet. The sum of money which she could take to a marriage settlement is mentioned in the very first sentence of the novel, and is the first fact to be learned about Maria. Money and chance in connection with marriage are mentioned again, in relation to the other sisters and their failure to secure such advantageous matches, when the narrator announces, 'there certainly are not so many men of large fortune in the world, as there are pretty women to deserve them.' This is a statement which, for wit and **ironic** worldliness, challenges the famous opening sentence of *Pride and Prejudice*: 'It is a truth universally acknowledged, that a single man in possession of a good fortune, must be in want of a wife.'

The voice of the narrator, or perhaps the **authorial voice** (see Narrative Modes) is evident in the opening passage of the novel, as Jane Austen, or her narrator, mocks the materialist view of marriage whilst seeming ruefully to accept it. The 'commendable' marriages of the two older sisters are described in terms of 'the greatness of the match' for Maria, and a 'career of conjugal felicity with very little less than a thousand a year' for Miss Ward, who has had a husband found for her by Sir Thomas, her brother-in-law.

The marriage of the youngest, Miss Frances – evidently an elopement – was, it seems, a love match, although the word 'love' is not mentioned, since the ironic **tone** of this passage is better suited by the suggestion that she married 'in the common phrase, to disoblige her family'. What is seen as the disgrace of her marriage to 'a Lieutenant of Marines, without education, fortune, or connections' might have been modified by the patronage of Sir Thomas, although it seems he had no influence in naval appointments, where 'no interest could reach', but the 'very imprudent' marriage led to a breach between Mansfield and Portsmouth.

The account of this breach gives the author an opportunity to sketch in the characters of the sisters and Sir Thomas, who will be the older generation of the main narrative. Sir Thomas is shown as ready to exert influence on behalf of those attached to him by marriage – partly from 'principle' but not least to improve the standing of a connection which he considers unsuitable. The unruffled inertia associated with Lady Bertram throughout the novel is outlined here in a positively-framed description – 'tranquil feelings, and a temper remarkably easy and indolent' – although the implication is of negative characteristics. The dangerous and malicious busybodying for which Mrs Norris will become notorious is forecast as she writes a spiteful letter to her newly-wed sister, in which the narrator points to her malevolent 'spirit of activity' which 'could not be satisfied', and how she 'threatens' her sister with 'possible ill consequences'. When Mrs Price replies with some invective in her turn, Mrs Norris 'could not possibly keep to herself' impolite comments about Lady Bertram and about Sir Thomas's pride.

The elegance of Jane Austen's prose can be seen at its height in this measured introduction. She was an admirer of the **balanced** style of Dr Samuel Johnson (1709–84), an example of whose **antithesis** is the basis of the final statement of Chapter 39: 'though Mansfield Park, might have some pains, Portsmouth could have no pleasures' (p. 325).

Several examples of balanced prose may be found in this opening passage, usually to humorous and ironic effect. The statement already noted, 'But there certainly are not so many men of large fortune in the world, as there are pretty women to deserve them', is an example of antithesis in the grand eighteenth-century style. Jane Austen uses balance in pairs of epithets or phrases, too, as in 'the comforts and consequences of an handsome house and large income'. Sir Thomas's pair of wishes, to act 'from principle as well as pride', are elaborated – and undermined – as 'from a general wish of doing right, and a desire of seeing all that were connected with him in situations of respectability'. Lady Bertram's 'indolent' nature is balanced in the same sentence with Mrs Norris's 'spirit of activity'.

There is **irony**, too, in the reference to Mansfield Park itself as a 'handsome house', and a few lines later to the two unmarried sisters as 'quite as handsome' as the baronet's bride. This has the effect of linking the young women with the house as though they too had the potential to become some kind of property – suggesting that a young woman's good looks could add to her husband's status.

This long opening paragraph manages – in smoothly constructed prose – to do considerably more than act as a prologue. The foundations of the narrative are laid, the characters of the older generation of the main story are sketched in, and the status of Sir Thomas Bertram of Mansfield Park is established. Furthermore, the **omniscient** but detached narrator lets the reader know what kind of novel this is: an ironic account of marriage in the genteel class of the time.

TEXT 2   (PAGES 107–9)

This passage ends Chapter 13 (Volume I, Chapter xiii). Lady Bertram is asleep on the sofa in the drawing room, and Fanny is sewing the difficult bits of her aunt's 'work', as Tom and Edmund discuss the proposed amateur dramatics. Tom has suggested that the entertainment would usefully distract his mother who, he says, is in a very anxious state about Sir Thomas's dangerous journey. This is belied by her peaceful repose, and Tom has to join in Edmund's amusement at the obviously unjustified claim. Edmund has explained his moral and ethical objections, which Tom has dismissed. At the beginning of the extract, Edmund tries a final argument, concerning the expense which such an 'Innovation' would incur.

"The Innovation if not wrong as an Innovation, will be wrong as an expense."

"Yes, the expense of such an undertaking would be prodigious! Perhaps it might cost a whole Twenty pounds.—Something of a Theatre we must have undoubtedly, but it will be on the simplest plan;—a green curtain and a little carpenter's work—and that's all; and as the carpenter's work may be all done at home by Christopher Jackson himself, it will be too absurd to talk of expense;—and as long as Jackson is employed, every thing will be right with Sir Thomas.—Don't imagine that nobody in this house can see or judge but yourself.—Don't act yourself, if you do not like it, but don't expect to govern every body else."

"No, as to acting myself," said Edmund, "*that* I absolutely protest against."

Tom walked out of the room as he said it, and Edmund was left to sit down and stir the fire in thoughtful vexation.

Fanny, who had heard it all, and borne Edmund company in every feeling throughout the whole, now ventured to say, in her anxiety to suggest some comfort, "Perhaps they may not be able to find any play to suit them. Your Brother's taste, and your Sisters', seem very different."

"I have no hope there, Fanny. If they persist in the scheme they will find something—I shall speak to my sisters and try to dissuade *them*, and that is all I can do."

"I should think my Aunt Norris would be on your side."

"I dare say she would; but she has no influence with either Tom or my Sisters that could be of any use; and if I cannot convince them myself, I shall let things take their course, without attempting it through her. Family squabbling is the greatest evil of all, and we had better do any thing than be altogether by the ears."

His sisters, to whom he had an opportunity of speaking the next morning, were quite as impatient of his advice, quite as unyielding to his representation, quite as determined in the cause of pleasure as Tom.—Their Mother had no objection to the plan, and they were not in the least afraid of their Father's disapprobation.—There could be no harm in what had been done in so many respectable families, and by so many women of the first consideration; and it must be scrupulousness run mad, that could see any thing to censure in a plan like theirs, comprehending only brothers and sisters, and intimate friends, and which would never be heard of beyond themselves. Julia *did* seem inclined to admit that Maria's situation might require particular caution and delicacy—but that could not extend to *her*—*she* was at liberty; and Maria evidently considered her engagement as only raising her so much more above restraint, and leaving her less occasion than Julia, to consult either Father or Mother. Edmund had little to hope, but he was still urging the subject, when Henry Crawford entered the room, fresh from the Parsonage, calling out, "No want of hands in our Theatre, Miss Bertram. No want of under strappers—My sister desires her love, and hopes to be admitted into the Company, and will be happy to take the part of any old Duenna or tame Confidante, that you may not like to do yourselves."

Maria gave Edmund a glance which meant, "What say you now? Can we be wrong if Mary Crawford feels the same?" And Edmund silenced, was obliged to acknowledge that the charm of acting might well carry fascination to the mind of Genius; and with the ingenuity of Love, to dwell more on the obliging, accommodating purport of the message than on any thing else.

The scheme advanced. Opposition was vain; and as to Mrs. Norris, he was mistaken in supposing she would wish to make any. She started no difficulties that were not talked down in five minutes by her eldest nephew and niece, who were all-powerful with her; and, as the whole arrangement was to bring very little expense to any body, and none at all to herself, as she foresaw in it all the comforts of hurry, bustle and importance, and derived the immediate advantage of fancying herself obliged to leave her own house, where she had been living a month at her own cost, and take up her abode in theirs, that every hour might be spent in their service; she was, in fact, exceedingly delighted with the project.

Tom, in his temporary position as head of the house, replies to Edmund's complaint in a high-handed way. He spurns the idea that expense will be 'prodigious!' – the exclamation mark underlining his sarcasm – and estimates it as 'a whole Twenty pounds' – that is, what he considers to be a trifling sum. The passionate nature of his speech (for this is a family row) is emphasised by the author's dashes as Tom invents points in favour of his plan, such as the advantage of having the estate carpenter fully employed. He attacks Edmund for what he sees as Edmund's self-righteous attitude: 'Don't imagine that nobody in this house can see or judge but yourself.'

Tom walks out – rudely, the reader infers – as Edmund confirms that he is implacably against acting in a play himself. He is left the loser in this battle between the brothers. The impetus of Tom's speech and his abrupt departure make it clear that he is likely to have his way.

Lady Bertram sleeps through the quarrel between her sons, so Fanny and Edmund are left virtually alone as Edmund, upset and annoyed, pokes the fire in frustration. Fanny, who has overheard the

exchange and suffered with Edmund, takes up her familiar role of
support, suggesting timidly that perhaps no suitable play will be found
(since her cousins are at odds over their preferences). Edmund believes
the only possible hope remaining lies in dissuading his sisters from acting;
he is already sensing defeat and does not believe that Mrs Norris is likely
to prevail either, although, as Fanny suggests, she might support his view.
Perhaps shaken by the fierceness of Tom's attack, he decides that, if he
fails with his sisters, he will take no further action, since 'family
squabbling' is to be avoided at all costs.

So far, the narrative in this extract has proceeded by means of **direct
speech**, which has forwarded the likelihood of the play being put on, and
has reinforced the reader's view of the characters. Tom's speech shows
him determined and forceful, rudely brushing aside his brother's
argument. The contrasting quiet exchange between Edmund and Fanny
shows them in agreement and at ease with each other; Fanny
demonstrates her sympathy for the defeated Edmund by trying to help;
Edmund has a chance to assess what is likely to happen and to prepare an
excuse – about family squabbling – if he has to give way finally.

The next paragraph demonstrates Jane Austen's use of what is often
called **free indirect speech,** in which the narrator's **voice** is fused with the
voices of the characters. In response to Edmund's strong objections to
acting, this device enables the two sisters to be represented at first as
speaking in a joint voice, arguing that Lady Bertram does not object, and
that neither would Sir Thomas; that other families did such things, and
so on. Then, Julia makes the case disingenuously for Maria's need for
greater discretion than herself, because of Maria's engagement to Mr
Rushworth; Maria counters that she is in fact independent and more
responsible for her own actions in her position as an engaged young
woman, and that Julia has the greater need to consult her parents about
the situation. This passage is able to give the effect, by means of free
indirect speech, of the jumbled and hasty arguments put forward
(unconvincingly, the reader might think) by the two girls as if speaking
in unison, following which their shared interest in Henry Crawford
divides them in their opposed analyses as to which of them should take
part in the play and which should abstain.

The wrangle ends as **direct speech** is resumed with Henry
Crawford's entrance. As usual, he brings extra life and energy to the

scene; here, he is described as 'calling out' the news of the enthusiasm at the Parsonage for the project, which will have 'no want of under strappers' (assistants). Mary Crawford is keen to join in and will take any humble part in which she might be useful. The lively good humour of the Crawfords and their social tact is much in evidence here.

In Edmund's eyes, Mary's willing acceptance extends support to the propriety of the projected theatricals. The narrator's voice takes over for the remainder of this extract, offering the reader the enjoyment of Edmund's justification of his changing views, now that he knows that Mary, with whom he is falling in love, is to be one of the players. The shift in his position is described in humorous terms, with a classical dimension – the **personification** of Genius in the last sentence of the paragraph represents the way in which Edmund describes Mary to himself, while Love is represented as the god who lets him see her as kind and obliging, whilst ignoring other aspects.

The final paragraph offers a vignette of the appalling Mrs Norris. Any hesitations she might feel over the plan are easily disposed of by Tom and Maria, who she has always spoilt, and the narrator shows Mrs Norris's delight in something which will pander to her self-importance, will cost her nothing, and in fact will profit her financially by her perceived need to move into Mansfield Park in order to busy herself there. Her meanness is underlined by the account of her having lived in her own house for just 'a month at her own cost'. The chapter ends with the unanticipated eager acceptance of the project by Mrs Norris, and the enterprise is under way.

It is noticeable that there is a rash of capitalisation in this excerpt – generally of nouns to do with the theatre – which may be intended to heighten the drama of the arguments (but see Note on the Text concerning the orthography of the selected text).

TEXT 3   (PAGES 341–2)

This extract, from Chapter 42 (Volume III, Chapter xi), begins when Henry Crawford, on an unexpected visit to Portsmouth, has escorted Fanny back to the Prices' house after the Sunday morning service and a walk on the ramparts. The rest of the family have gone inside to dinner, and Henry is making the most of a last few minutes alone with Fanny.

"I wish you were not so tired," said he, still detaining Fanny after all the others were in the house; "I wish I left you in stronger health.—Is there any thing I can do for you in town? I have half an idea of going into Norfolk again soon. I am not satisfied about Maddison.—I am sure he still means to impose on me if possible, and get a cousin of his own into a certain mill, which I design for somebody else.—I must come to an understanding with him. I must make him know that I will not be tricked on the south side of Everingham, any more than on the north, that I will be master of my own property. I was not explicit enough with him before.—The mischief such a man does on an estate, both as to the credit of his employer, and the welfare of the poor, is inconceivable. I have a great mind to go back into Norfolk directly, and put every thing at once on such a footing as cannot be afterwards swerved from.—Maddison is a clever fellow; I do not wish to displace him—provided he does not try to displace *me*;—but it would be simple to be duped by a man who has no right of creditor to dupe me—and worse than simple to let him give me a hard-hearted, griping fellow for a tenant, instead of an honest man, to whom I have given half a promise already—Would not it be worse than simple? Shall I go?—Do you advise it?"

"I advise!—you know very well what is right."

"Yes. When you give me your opinion, I always know what is right. Your judgment is my rule of right."

"Oh, no!—do not say so. We have all a better guide in ourselves, if we would attend to it, than any other person can be. Good bye; I wish you a pleasant journey to-morrow."

"Is there nothing I can do for you in town?"

"Nothing, I am much obliged to you."

"Have you no message for anybody?"

"My love to your sister, if you please; and when you see my cousin—my cousin Edmund, I wish you would be so good as to say that—I suppose I shall soon hear from him."

"Certainly; and if he is lazy or negligent, I will write his excuses myself—"

He could say no more, for Fanny would be no longer detained. He pressed her hand, looked at her, and was gone. *He* went to while away the next three hours as he could, with his other acquaintance, till the best dinner that a capital inn afforded, was ready for their enjoyment, and *she* turned in to her more simple one immediately.

Their general fare bore a very different character; and could he have suspected how many privations, besides that of exercise, she endured in her father's house, he would have wondered that her looks were not much more affected than he found them. She was so little equal to Rebecca's puddings, and Rebecca's hashes, brought to table as they all were, with such accompaniments of half-cleaned plates, and not half-cleaned knives and forks, that she was very often constrained to defer her heartiest meal, till she could send her brothers in the evening for biscuits and buns. After being nursed up at Mansfield, it was too late in the day to be hardened at Portsmouth; and though Sir Thomas, had he known all, might have thought his niece in the most promising way of being starved, both mind and body, into a much juster value for Mr. Crawford's good company and good fortune, he would probably have feared to push his experiment farther, lest she might die under the cure.

Fanny was out of spirits all the rest of the day. Though tolerably secure of not seeing Mr. Crawford again, she could not help being low. It was parting with somebody of the nature of a friend; and though in one light glad to have him gone, it seemed as if she was now deserted by everybody; it was a sort of renewed separation from Mansfield; and she could not think of his returning to town, and being frequently with Mary and Edmund, without feelings so near akin to envy, as made her hate herself for having them.

When emotions are not aroused, **direct speech** proceeds smoothly in the narrative: here both Fanny and the sophisticated Crawford are very aware of each other – Fanny disturbed and made nervous by his attentions, and Henry still determined to win her by making a good impression. Their speech is coherent, but the author indicates the underlying tension by dashes. Henry is fluent, as always; Fanny says little, although what she does say is to the point.

After expressing his anxiety about her health, Henry Crawford seeks to prolong the private interview by introducing a new topic, and one which will show him in a good light. The reader forms the impression, from the various ideas about his Norfolk estate which tumble out, that he is thinking on his feet as he proceeds with an account of problems with his bailiff. The many dashes reinforce this stopping-and-starting feel. Henry wants to be seen as a fair and competent manager of his estate, and one who cares about 'the welfare of the poor'. He is particularly anxious to avoid behaving in a 'simple' (meaning 'foolish') manner, and intends to flatter Fanny by asking her advice as to whether he should pay another visit to his estate, sooner than he had intended, to make sure everything is in order.

Fanny turns aside the compliment, but Henry shows his familiar persistence, saying, 'Your judgment is my rule of right.' He has employed this technique of asking for Fanny's advice and explanations at earlier points in the novel, in order to keep her in conversation (p. 283, for example). Henry, known to the reader for his acting skills and volatile nature, may well be acting a part here, although probably convincing himself of his sincerity. Fanny's thoughtful reply demonstrates her very real sincerity, however, when she says: 'We have all a better guide in ourselves, if we would attend to it, than any other person can be.'

This statement reminds the reader that Fanny has followed this precept herself throughout: she persisted in her belief that the private theatricals project was wrong, even when Edmund succumbed to pressure; and she has persisted in her refusal of Henry Crawford, which was not due to wilfulness, as Sir Thomas claimed, but to her knowledge that she could marry only for love. Perhaps, too, this speech marks an important stage in Fanny's growth to maturity – this is the statement of an independent woman, and of one who no longer has to rely on her cousin Edmund for guidance.

A short paragraph in the narrator's **voice** follows the exchange in **direct speech**: Henry tactfully avoids eating with the Prices in order not to embarrass Fanny and goes off to eat well with an acquaintance. Fanny goes indoors, out of the fresh air, to a very different kind of meal – the contrast between their expectations is marked by the italicised '*He*' and '*she*'. The narrative continues in a memorable paragraph about the horrors of Rebecca's cooking and table service, and the devastating effects on Fanny of 'being starved, both mind and body'; the final paragraph of this excerpt describes Fanny's low spirits and what she guiltily acknowledges as a wish to be elsewhere.

Jane Austen's ability to vary **narrative modes** (see Critical Approaches) is demonstrated at the end of the extract. In the paragraph beginning 'Their general fare' it is the narrator who speculates as to the thoughts of Henry Crawford and Sir Thomas if they could see Fanny's sufferings. Fanny, refined by Mansfield life to the point where she cannot cope with the rougher style of Portsmouth, is unable to eat until she can send out for something less squalid. In the final paragraph of this excerpt, however, the **narrative viewpoint** becomes Fanny's, as so often in the novel.

The style of the last two paragraphs is indicative of this narrative shift. In the first of the two, we recognise the **omniscient** and detached narrator in **balanced** statements such as: 'After being nursed up at Mansfield, it was too late in the day to be hardened at Portsmouth'; and 'he would probably have feared to push his experiment farther, lest she might die under the cure'. Heightened language to do with health is used: 'nursed', 'hardened', 'starved', 'die', 'cure' – perhaps as suggestive of struggling plant life as of a young woman's well-being. A considerable humour is present in the exaggeration and coolness of **tone**. The tone warms in the final passage, and the reader recognises that the narrative has shifted to Fanny's viewpoint. Real feelings are being described, and there is a human hesitancy of analysing thoughts evident in some of the language: 'she could not help', 'it seemed as if', 'it was a sort of'. This contrasts with the precision of expression of the narrator's voice.

This extract lies towards the end of the novel, but before the **peripeteia** (sudden reversal of fortunes) which leads to the resolution of the plot. Henry Crawford seems to be improving in his behaviour – his courtship is modest and tactful – and the reader wonders if Fanny, longing for escape from Portsmouth, might be softening towards him. He is, after all, in the context of marriage in the terms of the novel, an acceptably wealthy and attractive suitor. Still in love with Edmund, who appears to be on the point of proposing to Mary Crawford however, Fanny is seen to be at a pivotal point in the story, and the author keeps us guessing.

PART FIVE

BACKGROUND

JANE AUSTEN'S LIFE

EARLY DAYS

Jane Austen was born on 16 December 1775 in her father's country rectory in Steventon, Hampshire. She was the sixth child and second daughter of the Rev. George Austen and his wife, born Cassandra Leigh. There was to be one more son.

George Austen's grandfather had been a wealthy cloth merchant who fell upon hard times; his widow and children, including George's father, William, had to leave their Horsmonden manor house and remained the poor relations in the Austen family. However, William became a surgeon and, with the help of a prosperous relative, had his son, Jane Austen's father, educated at Oxford. The support shown by the wealthy towards struggling members of the family, not unusual at that time, is paralleled perhaps in Sir Thomas Bertram's assistance to the Price family.

Jane Austen's mother was the daughter of a Church of England clergyman with aristocratic connections, and niece of Theophilus Leigh, Master of Balliol (an Oxford college) for fifty years. The widespread family network, which covered a good deal of England and beyond, formed the setting for Jane Austen's life. The large families of the period and the many early deaths, which resulted in second and third marriages and more sets of step-relations, meant that family connections – kept up by correspondence and visits – could be very extensive.

Jane Austen's parents ran a boys' school at home in the rectory, where their sons were educated until they were at least twelve. Small Jane and her slightly older sister, Cassandra, would have been very much aware of the boys' noisy presence; the boarders, aged up to fourteen or fifteen, were always there, except for breaks at Christmas and in the summer. There must be an echo of those boisterous lads running about Jane Austen's home in Fanny Price's experiences of her rackety brothers at Portsmouth. Jane had five brothers: the eldest, James, followed his father to Oxford and succeeded him as Rector of Steventon. Her second brother, George, who did not live at Steventon, suffered from an undiagnosed illness, which afflicted him mentally and physically all his life. The next brother, Edward, was adopted by wealthy but childless relatives, the Knights, and inherited Godmersham Park in Kent. Parents of numerous offspring at that time often thought it an advantage to a child to be adopted or brought up by a much wealthier family – as in Fanny Price's removal to Mansfield Park. Henry Austen, the favourite brother, became a young man of great charm and various careers: he was first a captain in the Militia, later a London banker and finally, after his bank crashed, he was ordained and given a clerical living in the country by his rich brother – now Edward Knight. The other brothers, Frank and Charles, had successful naval careers, both rising to become admirals, after entering the navy at twelve, like William and Sam Price. They had many adventures in the Napoleonic Wars, and it is clear that Jane drew upon what she had learned of naval life from them for the nautical aspects of *Mansfield Park*. There is a direct parallel between the incident involving William's present of an amber cross to Fanny, and Charles's sending topaz crosses to his sisters, bought from his prize money after his ship was involved in the capture of a French vessel.

Jane's only sister, Cassandra, was about two years older than Jane, and they were always devoted to each other. Since the boys' school in the Rectory was seen as inappropriate, they were sent away to a small Oxford boarding school when Jane was seven. This school removed to Southampton, where Cassandra and Jane became ill with an infectious fever and were eventually taken home. There are few cheerful accounts of boarding schools of the period, and conditions were often harsh. Nevertheless, the girls were soon sent off again, this time to a school in Reading, where lessons were short and free time long. When Jane was eleven, her boarding school education ended and she went home, where her education continued on an informal basis: she studied French and Italian, learned to play the piano, and continued for the rest of her life the wide reading which had always been central to her tastes. Among her favourite authors were the novelists Henry Fielding, Laurence Sterne, Samuel Richardson and Fanny Burney, the essayist (and lexicographer) Samuel Johnson, whose style she much admired, and the poetry of George Crabbe, William Cowper and Walter Scott. Plays were sometimes put on by Jane's older brothers in the 1780s, the Rectory barn serving as a theatre. James, at that time studying at Oxford and seen as the writer of the family, provided skilful and topical prologues and epilogues. These activities, which had parental approval, represent one of the sources of the puzzle about Sir Thomas's disapproval of home theatricals in *Mansfield Park* – but see Social Background below.

Adult life

In 1801, the Rev. George Austen retired with his wife and daughters to lodgings in Bath. Jane, very fond of the Steventon Rectory, fainted when she heard they were to leave their home. She disliked Bath but enjoyed the summer travelling the family undertook to seaside places. There is a story, recounted by Cassandra in old age, that at one of the seaside towns they visited in Devon, her sister Jane developed a romantic interest in a young man who showed some signs of courting her. But, before the possibility of another summer meeting, they learned of his death. Biographer Claire Tomalin identifies another possible attachment which came to nothing: whilst Jane was still at Steventon, she met a young Irishman, Tom Lefroy, a relative of her brother James's in-laws. They met at a ball at Manydown, the manor home of friends the Bigg-Withers. Jane wrote several letters to Cassandra about this delightful young man, with whom she had much in common, including a shared interest in Fielding's *Tom Jones*. He agreed later in life that he had been in love with Jane Austen. However, at the time of the meetings, when Jane was twenty, young Lefroy had his way to make in the world, and must have been steered away by his family from involvement with a clergyman's penniless daughter.

Jane and Cassandra spent much of their time on visits to friends and relatives after leaving Steventon: in 1802, for instance, they spent eight weeks in Kent with their brother Charles and, on returning to pay visits in Hampshire, were invited to spend several weeks at Manydown. Here, Harris Bigg-Wither proposed to Jane, who he had known all his life. She accepted, amidst general approval. She would have become in time the mistress of a large house and estate – the kind of happy ending she planned for her heroines. But doubts crept in and the next morning she told Harris that she could not marry him, and left at once with Cassandra for Bath, to avoid further embarrassment. Jane was not, after all, to have the usual young woman's career of marriage and children. Her adventure in life was to be a very different one: no husband, but a gift for friendship; no children, but her novels, which she described as such. When she saw *Sense and Sensibility* finally in print, she said 'I can no more forget it, than a mother can forget her sucking child', and *Pride and Prejudice* was her 'darling child'.

Poor Cassandra had been engaged to a naval officer who died of fever in the West Indies in 1797. She and Jane were devoted and – rather too quickly, it was thought – gave up dancing and other pleasures of youth, and took on the characteristics of old maids. After 1805, the year of their father's death, there was a period of some hardship for George Austen's wife and daughters, with no church pension for them at that time. The loss of her father was a great blow to Jane, and life became very unsettled, as they had no real home of their own, endlessly visiting until the summer of 1809. Then, at last, the two sisters and their mother were offered a house by their wealthiest brother, Edward. The house was called a 'cottage', but was probably a one-time posting inn, with six bedrooms, gardens and outbuildings; and it was at Chawton, in the Austens' home county of Hampshire.

Jane, previously depressed and without a regular pattern of life, had written nothing for several years. Now, happily settled at Chawton, she was to write again and see her work published. She had no room of her own, but cheerfully worked on a table in the drawing room, where she could cover up her papers in the event of a visitor calling.

Her last years before her illness and death were busy and contented. Her large family and her friends experienced good and bad fortune, of course, and she shared in their happiness and grief. Chawton society was limited, but her visits continued – especially to Henry in London, where she enjoyed theatre visits and shops. She died whilst in Winchester on 18 July 1817, and was buried in the cathedral, where her memorial recognises her Christian qualities. It is often said that no mention is made on her tombstone of her life's work, but this is belied by the reference to 'the extraordinary endowments of her mind'.

Writing

Apart from her brother James's writing successes – he was published in his own magazine, *The Loiterer* (1789–91), and elsewhere – Jane's mother, Cassandra, was also talented. In spite of the daunting duties involved in running such a large household, not to mention a school, she sometimes dashed off humorous verses.

Jane herself was writing by the age of twelve: her recent biographer, Claire Tomalin, suggests in *Jane Austen: A Life* (1997) that these early stories are influenced by the boys' humour with which she was so familiar at home. In *Jack and Alice*, dedicated to her brother Francis, there are jokes about drunkenness, food, violent death and accidents, speculation about adult behaviour and rude remarks about personal appearances. Claire Tomalin writes: 'Jane Austen was a tough and unsentimental child, drawn to rude, anarchic imaginings and black jokes' (p. 30). Jane's subject matter changed and her style developed; her comical *History of England* (dated at the end '26 November, 1791') is full of family jokes and references. *Lesley Castle* (1792), a heartless **epistolary** story, focuses on a huge wedding banquet and the provision of food for it; food, of course, remains a subject of frequent reference in her major works. *Lesley Castle* is a scandalous tale of child abandonment, adultery and conversion to Roman Catholicism, topics which her Church of England father was able to appreciate in a spirit of literary criticism. He was a great admirer and encourager of his daughter's aspirations, taking care that she always had paper – an expensive item then – to write on.

Probably without her knowledge, her father sent her novel *First Impressions* (1797) to a publisher, who promptly turned it down: a serious misjudgement, since it was later published as *Pride and Prejudice*. She had also written an epistolary novel, *Elinor and Marianne*, which she rewrote as *Sense and Sensibility* in 1797–8; and *Lady Susan* (1798–9), later to be rewritten as *Northanger Abbey*, but not published until after her death, although a publisher had bought it in 1803.

It was not until 1811, when Jane Austen was thirty-five, that a novel was published: *Sense and Sensibility*. This proved to be a success, and was followed in 1813 by *Pride and Prejudice*.

There had been a break in Jane Austen's regular writing activity, probably due to her father's death in 1805 (she abandoned, unfinished, a novel called *The Watsons* in that year) and to an unsettled life. But, with a home again, and no doubt buoyed up by successful publication, she began *Mansfield Park* in 1811, *Emma* in 1814, *Persuasion* in 1816, and *Sanditon*, unfinished at her death, in 1817. *Mansfield Park* was the third of her novels to be published, the work of a confident and successful author. Her novels were published anonymously, but her authorship became an open secret, with her readership extending to court circles – the Prince Regent, who Jane detested, let it be known that he wished a work to be dedicated to him. Jane reluctantly dedicated *Emma* to the notorious Regent.

LITERARY BACKGROUND

Jane Austen's style owes most to the reasoned classicism of the eighteenth century; her themes – love, marriage, betrayal and loyalty – are traditional; her ironic stance delivers her comedies in the form of acute commentaries upon contemporary mores.

Generally, the prevailing balanced prose style of the so-called Age of Reason is what Jane Austen has adapted to her purpose. The weightiness of the style is particularly effective in its incongruity when applied to satire. A well-known example is Alexander Pope's *The Rape of the Lock* (1712), in which the poet's mock heroic style underlines the trivialities with which he is dealing, and this is also the style of Henry Fielding's mid-century political plays, moderated into something more suited to narrative in his novels, which he described as 'comic epics'. The eighteenth century saw the birth of the English novel in its recognisable form. Among those known as the 'fathers' of this form were Fielding, whose *Tom Jones* (1749) was a particular favourite, and Samuel Richardson, whose extended epistolary novels – the best-known is *Pamela, or Virtue Rewarded* (1740) – were models for some of Austen's early work.

Although her work was not published until 1811, by the end of the eighteenth century Austen had joined the proliferating novelists of the period – several of whom were women. But by this time classicism, which had long been the major identifying mode of the arts generally, had given way to Romanticism – and reason to sensibility. A somewhat loose term (as is classicism), Romanticism values emotion, individualism and concepts of freedom; the style is intense and imaginative; the landscape, the power of nature and the supernatural are central. The movement was widespread and its tenets followed in an artistic spectrum stretching from poetry to landscape gardening, as can be seen in *Mansfield Park*; the Romantic **Gothic novel** was very popular, its chief exponents towards the close of the century being 'Monk' Lewis (*The Monk*, 1796), William Beckford (*Vathek: an Arabian tale*, 1786), and Ann Radcliffe (*The Mysteries of Udolpho*, 1794). In these over-heated works, terror, passion and madness reigned amidst abductions to foreign castles, rapes, fires and tempests. These wild matters were not for Jane Austen, an early **realist**, although she used the genre to **satirical** purpose in *Northanger Abbey*: the heroine, Catherine Morland, steeped in Romantic Gothic novels, finally realises that it is not in the works of Radcliffe that 'human nature, at least in the midland counties of England, is to be looked for'. Austen often mocks concepts dear to Romanticism: sensibility itself, for instance; the Picturesque (see Settings); and even sensible Fanny Price suffers an attack of disappointed Romanticism in the chapel at Sotherton.

If Radcliffe's work is satirised in *Northanger Abbey*, other women writers were read with approval. The novels of 'manners' of Fanny Burney, who was in the court circle, and of Maria Edgeworth are identified as worthy examples. Fanny Burney was a favourite – her older women characters in *Cecilia* (1782) and *Evelina* (1778) make embarrassingly vulgar remarks, rather as Mrs Bennet does in *Pride and Prejudice*.

The novel was an increasingly popular form but also frequently despised by the seriously-minded as frivolous. In *Northanger Abbey* Jane Austen's narrator makes a well-known defence of what is 'only a novel', saying that a novel is 'only some work in which the greatest powers of the mind are displayed, in which the most thorough knowledge of human nature, the happiest delineation of its varieties, the liveliest effusions of wit and humour, are conveyed to the world in the best chosen language'.

Influenced as she was by admired writers, particularly of the eighteenth century, but reacting against the excesses of Romanticism, Jane Austen's work remains unique. With no need for wider literary ambitions and with a highly sophisticated writing technique, she is perhaps the first virtuoso of the form of the novel itself.

Jane Austen herself kept to the advice she gave her would-be novelist niece, to limit her characters and settings to a few families in a country village. It was not her intention to deal with a wider horizon. Nevertheless, some national and international events do form a relevant background to *Mansfield Park* (see also Chronology), especially in support of the claim that it is a novel about the state of the nation.

A BROAD

Austen lived in an era of revolution and war: the American War of Independence was fought during her childhood, and the French Revolution – the clearest manifestation of the thinking of **Romanticism** – began when she was in her teens. England's subsequent wars with France and French allies continued until almost the end of Jane Austen's life. There was an Irish rebellion, and wars in India from the end of the eighteenth century. Fanny Price's brother William, in *Mansfield Park*, had 'known every variety of danger, which sea and war together could offer' (p. 196), and the dangers to which Sir Thomas was exposed on his voyage to Antigua and back were not only the usual perils of seagoing at that time, but also those of attack by enemy ships.

A T HOME

If the world beyond England was in a state of turbulence, matters at home were not altogether stable either. In 1811, when Austen began *Mansfield Park*, King George III suffered his final, irreversible attack of madness and the Prince of Wales became Regent, formally established in 1812. The Prince Regent was a leader of fashion and a patron of the arts, but was a notorious figure who treated his wife, Princess Caroline, very badly – arousing Jane Austen's sympathy for this rather dubious lady. The Prince had returned to his long-term mistress, Mrs Fitzherbert, soon after his marriage and was known for other very public liaisons. He was also outrageously extravagant in his private and public spending at a time, during the Napoleonic Wars, when there was much hardship amongst the poor, and financial anxiety amongst the wealthier classes – Sir Thomas's visit to Antigua is as a result of falling income. In 1812 the prime minister, Spencer Perceval, was assassinated in the lobby of the

House of Commons by a distraught bankrupt broker. At the same time, Luddite workers, afraid that industrial advances would mean the loss of their jobs, began to smash up the modern weaving and knitting frames in Northern and Midland counties.

There is undoubtedly a dark tone to *Mansfield Park*, noted by its earliest readers, and a sense that things have gone wrong, that Mansfield Park, which should stand for solid worth and respectability, has become destabilised. But then, beyond the constraints of the narrative, madness had struck down a virtuous king, a licentious and extravagant prince had become head of state, and the prime minister had been murdered in the House of Commons. The troubles that afflict the Bertram family may well be seen as an infection which has spread down from the top – from London, specifically, which in *Mansfield Park* is seen as the source of all evil (see Settings).

THE SLAVE TRADE

In recent years critics have been alert to the fact that Jane Austen lived in a slave-owning society. This is historically evident; the slave trade was abolished by British law in 1807–8, and the final, legal emancipation of slaves in the Empire did not come about until the 1830s. There cannot have been many families of even moderate prosperity who had no connections with slavery. In 1760, Jane Austen's father himself took up the trusteeship of a plantation in Antigua. In *Mansfield Park*, Fanny Price's question about the slave trade and the silence that followed have recently been the source of much speculation, particularly by **post-colonialist** critics (see Recent Criticism for further analysis).

SOCIAL BACKGROUND

The wars and other international troubles and the hardship at home did not impinge a great deal upon the everyday lives of country gentlemen and their families, although wages fell drastically for agricultural workers. As always in wartime, fortunes were made and lost and there might be less dramatic financial stringencies for some, such as those experienced by Sir Thomas Bertram, who seemed to find himself more dependent than usual on his income from Antigua.

FASHIONABLE LIFE

Fashion in all things was led by the Prince of Wales, later the Prince Regent. In spite of his political shortcomings and notorious private life, he left a legacy of what is called 'Regency' style, which is marked by changes in architecture and landscape gardening, in dress and in public entertainment.

While still Prince of Wales, and with his friend 'Beau' Brummel, he made it essential for the fashionable to spend time each year at the spa town of Bath, taking advantage of the medicinal waters, promenading and attending concerts, balls and lectures. Jane Austen's father retired there in 1801, and the writer disliked the place, preferring the less intense pleasures of Cheltenham Spa when she felt the need to take a 'cure'. Bath features often in her novels, in *Mansfield Park* less so, although Mrs Rushworth tactfully leaves home when her son is married, and goes to the spa town. There are anxieties about Fanny Price's health and complexion when she is exiled to Portsmouth, but, patronised by the Prince, other seaside towns such as Brighton, where the Prince had the famous Pavilion built, became fashionable for the first time. Horse racing had been a royal hobby since the days of Charles II, and the Prince Regent owned some of the finest horses in the country. The pleasures of racing are reflected in *Mansfield Park*, when Tom Bertram goes off with a promising horse he intends to run. Ladies rode for their health, as do the Bertram girls, Mary Crawford and Fanny in the novel.

THE THEATRE AND AMATEUR THEATRICALS

In London, much musical and theatrical entertainment, some of it in the open air, was available to those who could pay. We learn in *Mansfield Park* that both Lady Bertram and her sister had enjoyed theatre-going when they were younger, and Edmund – who is to enter the Church – refers to his theatre visits and the fact that he has seen a performance of *Lovers' Vows*. Jane Austen's own brothers put on plays as young men, and Tom points out that Sir Thomas used to approve of the Bertram sons' learning and reciting speeches at one time. A pleasure in amateur theatricals, however, is what divides the unprincipled characters at Mansfield from the virtuous, and Sir Thomas's total disapproval of such activities, foreseen and supported by Edmund and Fanny, seems to some critics like a great deal of fuss about nothing. So, what are the objections? Obviously, Sir Thomas does not like his house to be disarranged; but his disapproval goes deeper, and the first key to understanding why lies in his attitude to the Hon. John Yates. Unlike the upper-middle-class Sir Thomas and his circle, Yates is an aristocrat, and has come to Mansfield from an interrupted theatrical party at an aristocratic house. Sir Thomas detests him, as is registered when Yates leaves the house, with all hope of theatricals at an end: 'Sir Thomas hoped in seeing him out of it, to be rid of the worst object connected with the scheme, and the last that must be inevitably reminding him of its existence' (p. 163). This dislike may well be connected with the fact that amateur theatricals had become, at the beginning of the nineteenth century, a popular pastime of the more raffish aristocracy, and this would influence the respectable baronet against such goings-on. In 1802 for example, Albinia, Countess of Buckinghamshire, formed a group known as the Pic Nic Society (because, following the French custom, all members brought a contribution of food to meetings). The Picknickers, managed by Colonel Henry Greville, not only put on plays – in English and French – but rehearsed, scandalously, on Sundays. The Prince of Wales's current mistresses, Lady Jersey and Mrs Fitzherbert, played leading roles; Lady Albinia herself, in addition to her interest in food and drama, ran a notoriously crooked gambling club. It is not hard to see that, subsequently, amateur theatricals had developed a reputation for impropriety, and that sons and – in particular – daughters of the respectable upper-middle class would attract opprobrium in taking part.

DRESS

In the aftermath of the French Revolution, dress changed dramatically: the extravagant styles of the eighteenth century gave way to a simple elegance, or even to austerity in those who wished to recognise the principles of the Revolution. Some members of the upper classes thought it prudent to modify their style of dress to avoid any suggestion of affinity with those who had been violently overthrown in France. Men no longer wore wigs or powdered their hair; buckles and fancy trimmings gave way to an elegant outline; and black, or dark colours, were favoured. Dress etiquette was strict, however, and the arbiters of taste were the Prince and 'Beau' Brummel. Young women, such as Jane and Cassandra Austen – and Jane Austen's heroines – constantly risked chills, since the neoclassical style adopted was typically a loose, flimsy, light-coloured dress, caught in below the breasts, which were generously exposed. Older women wore the same style, but usually in a more substantial fabric. At evening balls or public events a long feather or two arranged above a light turban – or some variation on this theme – was usual. Bonnets were daytime wear. As in the case of men, there was a striking change in hair style. The hair was worn up, usually with a curled fringe around the forehead (as in the well-known watercolour drawing of Jane Austen by her sister). Gone were the long tresses and ringlets that had hung down around the head; in what seemed to some a macabre reference to the victims of the guillotine, the neck was left bare.

Domestic life

The aristocracy remained a small, fairly impenetrable elite, who often lived very splendidly, employing regiments of servants and estate workers. For the gentry, too, to the lower reaches of which Jane Austen's family belonged, domestic life was greatly eased by the work of servants. Mansfield Park, the home of more prosperous gentry, obviously has a large number of servants, though few are identified. The butler, probably not right at the top of the hierarchy of servants, is mentioned as a good fire-builder; in addition to his duties in ensuring that the fires in the reception rooms were all burning well, he would make regular checks that everything was in place, draw the blinds as necessary, and see that newspapers were cut and aired. He would also look after the wine and take charge of the dining room. Lady Bertram's maid, identified as 'Chapman', would have been required to brush her mistress's hair and put it in curling papers at bedtime, apply cosmetics and skin lotions, as well as looking after Lady Bertram's clothes and dressing and undressing her.

With servants to do everything practical, the ladies of the house, in particular, were left with many idle hours. The men had interests in their estates and in energetic outdoor activities. Their wives and sisters led a mainly indoor life, especially in a bad winter when, as Jane Austen put it in a letter, it was not fit for a 'female foot' to venture out, although the well-booted men could do so. The visits to stay with distant relatives and friends, or local trips to neighbours, were a central part of Austen's life, and they are looked forward to by the characters of *Mansfield Park*.

MARRIAGE

For most women of the class with which Austen is concerned there was no future development open to them but marriage and the upbringing of children. In fact, in *Mansfield Park*, Sir Thomas, Lady Bertram and Maria all express in one way or another that it is the duty of a woman to accept a 'good' offer of marriage. Fanny, like Jane herself, is unusual in that she turns down the prospect of a financially secure future, because of a lack of love. Such a refusal could be seen as reckless, since an unmarried woman would be dependent, as Jane Austen was for much of her life, on support from relatives. The only acceptable alternative was to become a governess – an often uncomfortable position in which genteel status was in peril. Needless to say, Austen's own career was unusual, and only just becoming respectable – even so, she took the precaution of publishing all her work anonymously.

THE CHURCH

Church-going had diminished in the eighteenth century – the Age of Reason – and absentee clergymen had been easy subjects for **satire**. The events of the French Revolution produced a change of heart, and church-going resumed a central place in society at the end of the century. Reforms were afoot: although in 1780 a quarter of the 10,000 parishes in England had no resident parson, a Bill of 1808 required all clergymen to live in their parishes. That this was not altogether the case at the time of *Mansfield Park* seems clear, since Edmund appears to choose rather than be obliged to live in the parish which his father allocates to him.

By this time, there were fewer indigent clergy; Jane Austen's own father had a comfortable income (although the Church later made no provision for his widow and unmarried daughters).

Several nonconformist groups – such as the Quakers and the Methodists – were to become popular movements as the nineteenth century progressed. The Evangelicals, or 'Saints', of whom the anti-slavery campaigner William Wilberforce was a leading member, were, however, generally supported by the more genteel classes at the beginning of the century. It has been suggested that Fanny Price may have been an Evangelical (see Recent Criticism), although Jane Austen herself seems to have been sceptical. She wrote to her sister after a church service that she did not much like the new sermons: 'They are fuller of Regeneration and Conversion than ever.'

PART SIX

CRITICAL HISTORY & BROADER PERSPECTIVES

EARLIER RESPONSES

FIRST OPINIONS

The first, three-volume, edition of *Mansfield Park* of about 1,250 copies sold out in six months. The author's profits were £350, much to the delight of Jane Austen, who had no income of her own.

There were no published reviews of *Mansfield Park*, but Austen collected and wrote down opinions which she received in correspondence or conversation. There was frequent praise, including that of the publisher, Thomas Egerton, for the novel's 'morality'. The 'sound treatment' of the clergy is mentioned, as well as the examination of the flaws in contemporary education, and the high principles of the heroine were applauded.

But not all views of the novel were favourable; some of the opinions that Austen recorded show that her readers were disconcerted by the ending of the narrative and by the failure of the dashing Crawford to win the heroine. Fanny herself was often disliked – seen as no match for Elizabeth Bennet in *Pride and Prejudice*, for instance. Austen's nearest relatives were more discreet in their judgements, although her forthright mother described Fanny as 'insipid'.

A GROWING REPUTATION

Jane Austen hoped that Sir Walter Scott, whose historical novels and verse she much admired, would include a review of *Mansfield Park* when he wrote about her next published novel, *Emma*, in the *Quarterly Review* (Vol. xiv, 1815, which apparently pre-dated publication of *Emma*). He did not mention *Mansfield Park* specifically, but offered somewhat modest praise for the **realism** of her work generally: 'The narrative of all her novels is composed of such common occurrences as may have fallen under the observation of most folks; and her *dramatis personæ* conduct themselves upon the motives and principles which the readers may recognize as ruling their own and that of most of their acquaintances.' Later, after Austen's death – although still referring to her as 'that young lady' – he came to a greater appreciation of her talent, directed as it was towards such a different narrative goal from his own. In an entry in his diary for March 1826, Scott wrote of Jane Austen:

> [She] has a talent for describing the involvements and feelings and characters of ordinary life, which is to me the most wonderful I have ever met with. The Big Bow-Wow strain I can do myself like any now going; but the exquisite touch which renders common-place things and characters interesting from the truth of the description and sentiment is denied to me.

It was the publication of nephew James Edward Austen-Leigh's memoirs of Jane Austen in 1870 which led to her wider popularity and prompted much more general critical interest. By the end of the nineteenth century many publishers had put out editions of her major novels, which have never subsequently been out of print.

CRITICS AT LOGGERHEADS

Throughout most of its critical history, *Mansfield Park*, as with other works of Austen, has tended to generate a polarisation of views, with supporters and detractors lining up perhaps predictably and, in the case of her detractors, writing with some virulence. Attacked by Charlotte Brontë and Elizabeth Barrett Browning for what they saw as a limiting lack of expression of emotion or passionate feeling, Austen's work was spurned by the Americans Mark Twain and Ralph Waldo Emerson as tedious, and thought 'snobbish', amongst other things, by D.H. Lawrence. In 1970 one of our most successful modern writers of comedy, Kingsley Amis, in the first essay of *Whatever Became of Jane Austen?* begins with an appreciation of Austen's technical skills, to which he acknowledges a twentieth-century debt. This soon turns into a much-quoted analysis of Edmund and Fanny as impossibly dull: 'to invite Mr and Mrs Edmund Bertram round for the evening would not be lightly undertaken'. Worse, he finds them both 'morally detestable' and Fanny 'a monster of complacency and pride who, under a cloak of cringing self-abasement, dominates and gives meaning to the novel'.

Some of Jane Austen's supporters have included the Victorian novelist George Eliot and her partner, the writer G.H. Lewes, who admired Austen but saw her work as likely to appeal to an intellectual elite, within 'a small circle of cultivated minds'. Novelists as diverse as Henry James and Rudyard Kipling have been admirers of Jane Austen; the latter wrote a short story, *The Janeites* (1936), which identifies and celebrates a supportive Austen cult.

A now little-known novelist, Julia Kavanagh, perceptively identified in 1862 a dark strain in Austen's works which is particularly evident in *Mansfield Park*: 'If we look into the shrewdness and quiet satire of her stories, we shall find a much keener sense of disappointment than joy fulfilled.'

There is no doubt that *Mansfield Park* is a difficult work at any level beyond its surface wit and narrative flow. One of the most influential commentaries on the novel earlier this century was the essay by the liberal humanist critic Lionel Trilling (1905–75). This is included in his collection *The Opposing Self* (1955), and is a complex and wide-ranging analysis of various aspects of *Mansfield Park*. In the course of the essay, he deals with the concept of the 'self', and this is helpful in analysing the central female characters of Fanny Price and Mary Crawford. 'Nobody', Trilling writes, 'has ever found it possible to like the heroine of *Mansfield Park*.' She is too sickly and too virtuous, maybe, for our tastes, perhaps because her virtue does not have to battle against any tendency to sin. Mary Crawford, however, is 'all pungency and wit. Her mind is as lively and competent as her body; she can bring not only a horse but a conversation to a gallop.' Yet, Trilling explains, Jane Austen intends us to reject the vital Mary in favour of Fanny, who is part of the late eighteenth- and early nineteenth-century tradition of the physically frail, Christian heroine. Mary's extreme liveliness belongs to 'the world, the flesh and the devil'.

Although this explanation is perfectly acceptable, it may not lead to a switch in preferences between Fanny and Mary, particularly in the view of late twentieth-century readers. However, Trilling's comments on the nature of the integrity of the 'self' in relation to the novel provide food for thought. He suggests that Mary's fashionable style needs to be set against Fanny's sincerity when we are making judgements about the two women. It does seem that it is Fanny's almost oppressive sincerity that gives her weight as a heroine. The more often *Mansfield Park* is re-read, Trilling claims, the less appealing Mary's conversation appears. Today, Mary Crawford would no doubt be described in terms of a 'lifestyle', adaptable to the latest fashion, and thereby fragmenting the concept of 'self'; Fanny's character, by contrast, grows consistently from a 'self' which maintains its integrity.

Commentaries which pre-date 1938 by those mentioned above and many others are collected in Brian Southam's comprehensive work *Jane Austen: The Critical Heritage* (see Further Reading).

RECENT CRITICISM

In spite of some critical reservations, the critical comments mentioned above have on the whole been directed towards the delights of Austen's text and the effects of her characterisation on readers' susceptibilities. More recent developments in literary criticism have focused on different cultural insights into her work.

The work of many contemporary critics follows a reaction against the **New Criticism** of the earlier part of the twentieth century. The supporters of the New Criticism stressed the aesthetic inviolability of a work of art – for instance, a poem should be studied as a poem, a novel as a novel, and not for other than aesthetic reasons. Some of the critics who have rejected the aesthetic constraints of the New Criticism are identified by David Lodge in *After Bakhtin* (1990) as discovering a classic **realist** text, such as *Mansfield Park*, to be 'an instrument of ideology, a genre founded on bad faith, on the pretence that bourgeois culture is "natural", using the dominance of the authorial voice … to limit meaning in the interests of control, repression and privilege'. He also agrees that Jane Austen accepted 'the existence of class society (although she did not see it as fixed or static), that she subscribed to the Christian–humanist notion of the autonomy and responsibility of the individual self, and that her novels unequivocally endorse certain values and reject others.'

David Lodge himself does not believe that these are grounds for condemnation, and argues for a return to 'a reaffirmation of the writer's creative and communicative power', and deplores what he sees as 'a barrier of non-comprehension between academic and non-academic discussion of literature'. (David Lodge quotations are from Chapter 8 of *After Bakhtin*.)

However, the concept of the classic realist novel as 'an instrument of ideology' is that which is explored by **post-structuralist** critics, and this is the premiss on which **New Historicist** and **feminist** literary criticism relevant to *Mansfield Park* is founded.

To some of these critics, in **deconstructing** her texts, what Jane Austen does not say is even more revealing than what she does. The examination of what are seen as gaps in the overall narrative is one application of deconstruction – the revelation of hidden or partially hidden meanings in a text. Austen set her own constraints upon her intentions as a novelist, but critics have nevertheless often pointed to supposed deficiencies: there is no mention of the wars and revolutions which were the background to her life, or of political events nationally; no sex or passion in stories about love and marriage. For modern critics re-reading classic texts, these perceived absences have a great significance. An extreme example of this approach may be seen in Warren Roberts's *Jane Austen and the French Revolution* (1979), in which he claims that, since Austen never mentions such a momentous event as the French Revolution, it can be identified as a brooding preoccupation in the background of her novels.

NEW HISTORICISM

A more sustainable argument is put forward in Edward Said's **post-colonial** work, *Culture and Imperialism*, 1993. This is a much-admired and wide-ranging account of the way in which colonialist attitudes are embedded in English literature – not only, he claims, in relation to the twentieth and late nineteenth centuries, but back into the eighteenth century. He focuses in particular on *Mansfield Park* in relation to Jane Austen's work. That the novel is a 'state of the nation' work is a widespread view. Edward Said, in a key development in Austen criticism, demonstrates that the problems of the status and role of Mansfield Park, as an indicator of the condition of England, can be understood only when Mansfield Park itself is observed in relation to other places – in England and abroad. Mansfield must be seen in relation to London,

Portsmouth and the West Indies. The dislocations of the novel are crucial for Said:

- first, Fanny is displaced from Portsmouth to Mansfield, then exiled from Mansfield to Portsmouth, before returning triumphant

- next, there are the Crawfords' journeys, carrying a kind of infection between London and Mansfield

- finally, and particularly, there are Sir Thomas's voyages to Antigua and back.

These dislocations are seen as forming the structure of the novel and forwarding its key events. From his post-colonialist viewpoint, Edward Said focuses on the Antiguan element and the author's acceptance of the concept of the West Indies not as countries in themselves, but as outlying agricultural and manufacturing estates of the English gentry, maintained, of course, by slave labour.

The malaise at Mansfield Park, manifested by Sir Thomas's idle wife, malign sister-in-law and unsatisfactory daughters and heir, may be seen, as by many critics, to be the direct extension of corruption in high places – the taint brought by the amoral Crawfords and Yates. The re-establishment at Mansfield Park of stability and order requires moral and financial rescue from outside. As Edward Said explains, Austen's final, ironic restoration of all the deserving to a state of 'tolerable' comfort has depended on two external factors, energising the continuance of Mansfield Park: Fanny and her principled outlook is 'brought in' from Portsmouth, and Sir Thomas, his travels over, 'brings in' from Antigua the means to maintain the status of Mansfield Park.

Edward Said's theories have been seen as an attack on Jane Austen: he says, 'Yes, Austen belonged to a slave owning society', and claims that the Bertrams (and, by implication, Austen's other wealthy characters) 'could not have been possible without the slave trade, sugar and the colonial planter class'. He also suggests that *Mansfield Park* is 'about order at home and slavery abroad', implying that the first is maintained at the expense of the latter. However, forthright as his New Historicist approach is, he does not lack appreciation for Austen's brilliance as a novelist. In fact, he stresses that the reader's task is 'to lose neither a true historical sense' of the implicit background, nor the enjoyment of her literary skills – 'all the while seeing both together'. (Edward Said quotations are from 'Jane Austen and Empire', Chapter 2, Part II of *Culture and Imperialism*.)

FEMINIST CRITICISM

Recent feminist critics have usually taken for granted a politicised view of *Mansfield Park*, although their varying interpretations bear witness to the complexity of the possibilities that the novel offers. Marilyn Butler, for instance, in 'Mansfield Park: Ideology and Execution', from her influential *Jane Austen and the War of Ideas* (1975), reads the subtext of the novel as strongly supporting the conservative establishment and the social dimension of the Church of England, thus opposing the views of the 'Jacobins' or radicals. A diametrically opposed reading has been offered more than once, however. This posits the shakiness of the hierarchical social structure's dependence on an insecure middle class, as illustrated in the instability of Mansfield Park – the patriarchal direction of the education of the young Bertrams demonstrates its shortcomings. Also, of course, there is a challenge to Anglicanism in the Evangelical tendencies of Fanny.

The irony of the much-discussed ending can be interpreted as supporting either view: the ending can be seen as accepting, albeit a little cynically, that comfortable conservative values will prevail; or it can be argued that the marked undercutting of the closure by Austen's heavy irony is tantamount to a rallying cry for democratic change.

Many critics recognise the escape that authorship offered to Jane Austen from the conventions and restraints that beset women of her class; the creation of lively but unprincipled characters such as Mary Crawford could even offer vicarious opportunities of outrageous behaviour. This form of escape into fulfilment and rebellion against the strict limits set by society was, of course, rare.

Education is now regarded as the crucial element in the formation and acceptance of the woman's role at the time. Jane Austen herself is seen to be critical of the education of Maria and Julia in *Mansfield Park*, and Sir Thomas, at the end of the narrative, is made to recognise that 'his cares had been directed to the understanding and manners, not the disposition; and of the necessity of self-denial and humility, he feared they had never heard from any lips that could profit them' (p. 382). Fanny herself seems to exemplify a better kind of education, seemingly that approved by the author. Childhood hardship (in Portsmouth) is valued as character-forming; Fanny is ignorant and unaccomplished in her cousins' eyes, but she reads widely and observes life. In the style of the *Bildungsroman*, she gains in confidence and reaches social maturity by the end of the novel.

However, Ruth Bernard Yeazell argues in her essay 'The Boundaries of *Mansfield Park*' (1984) that Fanny's is actually a character fully formed from the start. She lacks social assurance but never hesitates in her judgements: she is right about the theatricals, and her assessment of Henry Crawford's character is exact – it is Edmund and Sir Thomas who have lessons to learn about Henry's irresponsibility. Yeazell sees Fanny's short history not as a story about growing up, or about education in its broadest sense, but as being about a Cinderella-like girl in a fairy story, 'a myth of recognition, a fantasy of being at last acknowledged for the princess one truly is'.

You will want to test some of the many critical ideas, a few of which have been outlined above, against your own close reading and re-reading of *Mansfield Park*. As you can see, some views will sit more or less comfortably side by side; others, however, are mutually exclusive.

FURTHER READING

Jane Austen's works may be found in many editions, including paperbacks. The six novels, in original order of publication, are *Sense and Sensibility*, *Pride and Prejudice*, *Mansfield Park*, *Emma*, *Persuasion* and *Northanger Abbey*. Many recent editions, including the selected text for this Note, have up-to-date commentaries in their introductions and useful notes. The authoritative editions are still those of R.W. Chapman, in Volumes I–V of *The Oxford Illustrated Jane Austen* (Oxford University Press), the most recent editions of which were published in the 1960s and 1970s. Volume VI, *Minor Works*, includes Austen's juvenilia, early versions of her major novels and unfinished work.

LETTERS

Jane Austen was a consistent and accomplished correspondent. In particular, she wrote frequently to her sister Cassandra whenever they were parted, even if only for a day or two. Unfortunately for posterity, Cassandra did her duty according to the custom of the time and destroyed or censored her sister's letters after Jane's death. What Cassandra considered unlikely to give offence remains, and forms the bulk of her surviving correspondence, collected and edited by R.W. Chapman in *Jane Austen's Letters* (Oxford University Press, 1932). The latest edition – also available in paperback – is edited by Deirdre Le Faye, 1995.

BIOGRAPHIES

The first account of Jane Austen's life was written by her nephew, James-Edward Austen-Leigh, and published by Bentley in 1870: *A Memoir of Jane Austen* is a discreet account of her life, with material about the Austen family gathered by her nephew and his sisters. There have been many biographies published in the twentieth century, some informatively illustrated, such as Marghanita Laski's *Jane Austen and Her World* (Thames and Hudson, 1969). The most recent account, which includes some critical commentary, is Claire Tomalin's *Jane Austen: A Life* (Viking, 1997). This is a detailed account of Jane Austen's life, which includes an analysis of some of the harsher aspects of her circumstances, and the ways in which she met them.

CRITICISM

Critical writing about Jane Austen's works up until the end of the 1930s is collected and edited in Brian C. Southam's *Jane Austen: The Critical Heritage* (Routledge and Kegan Paul, 1968, 1987); Volume I covers 1811–70, and Volume II covers 1870–1938.

There is great deal of recent commentary on Jane Austen, and on *Mansfield Park* itself. The following brief list offers useful starting points and includes some texts mentioned in this Note.

Isobel Armstrong, *Mansfield Park*, Penguin Critical Studies, 1988

Marilyn Butler, *Jane Austen and the War of Ideas*, Oxford, 1975 (revised 1987)

Moira Ferguson, 'Mansfield Park: Slavery, Colonialism and Gender', in the *Oxford Literary Review*, No. 13, 1991

Barbara Hardy, *A Reading of Jane Austen*, Peter Owen, London, 1975

David Lodge, 'Composition, distribution, arrangement: Form and structure in Jane Austen's novels', Chapter 8 of *After Bakhtin*, Routledge, 1990

Warren Roberts, *Jane Austen and the French Revolution*, Macmillan, 1979; paperback edition, Athlone Press, 1995

Edward W. Said, 'Jane Austen and Empire', Chapter 2, Part II of *Culture and Imperialism*, Chatto and Windus, 1993

John Sutherland, 'Where does Sir Thomas's wealth come from?', in *Is Heathcliff A Murderer? Puzzles in 19th-Century Fiction*, Oxford, 1996

Tony Tanner, *Jane Austen*, Macmillan, 1986

Lionel Trilling, *The Opposing Self*, Secker and Warburg, 1955

Andrew H. Wright, *Jane Austen's Novels: A Study in Structure*, Pelican, 1972

Ruth Bernard Yeazell, 'The Boundaries of *Mansfield Park*', in *Representations*, No. 7, 1984

World events	Jane Austen's life	Literature
		1740 Samuel Richardson, *Pamela, or Virtue Rewarded*
		1749 Henry Fielding, *The History of Tom Jones, a Foundling*
		1755 Samuel Johnson, *A Dictionary of the English Language*
		1757 John Home, *Douglas, A Tragedy*
		1758-60 Samuel Johnson writes *The Idler* series of essays
1760 George III accedes to the throne	**1760** George Austen, Jane Austen's father, takes up trusteeship of a plantation in Antigua	
		1768 Laurence Sterne, *A Sentimental Journey Through France and Italy*
1770 Captain James Cook discovers Botany Bay, Australia		
		1771 Oliver Goldsmith, *A History of England;* Henry Mackenzie, *The Man of Feeling*
1773 The 'Boston Tea Party': workers in Boston protest against British attempts to tax the American Colonies		
1775-6 American War of Independence breaks out, following the thirteen rebel colonies' declaration of independence from Britain	**1775** Birth of Jane Austen at Steventon, Hampshire	
1777 France officially joins the Americans in the war against Britain		
		1778 Fanny Burney, *Evelina*
		1782 Fanny Burney, *Cecilia*

World events	Jane Austen's life	Literature
1783 American independence is finally recognised by Britain in the Treaty of Paris, ending the war		**1783** Hugh Blair, *Lectures on Rhetoric and Belles-Lettres*
		1784 Death of Samuel Johnson
		1785 William Cowper, *The Task*
		1786 William Beckford, *Vathek: an Arabian Tale*
1788 George III's first attack of madness		**1788** First edition of *The Times* newspaper
1789 Outbreak of the French Revolution; George Washington becomes first president of the United States of America		
	1791-2 The young Jane Austen writes *History of England* and *Lesley Castle* (both unpublished)	**1791** James Boswell, *The Life of Johnson*
1792 France is declared a republic		
1793 France declares war on Britain during the ongoing French Revolutionary Wars; execution of Louis XVI and Marie Antoinette		
		1794 Ann Radcliffe, *The Mysteries of Udolpho;* William Blake, *Songs of Innocence and Experience;* Prince Hoare, *My Grandmother*
		1796 Matthew 'Monk' Lewis, *The Monk*
	1797 *First Impressions* is rejected for publication; later rewritten as *Pride and Prejudice*	
	1797-8 An earlier work, *Elinor and Marianne,* is rewritten as *Sense and Sensibility*	

World events	Jane Austen's life	Literature
	1798-9 Jane Austen writes *Lady Susan* (unpublished; later rewritten and published as *Northanger Abbey*)	**1798** *Lovers' Vows*, an adaptation by Elizabeth Inchbald of August von Kotzebue's *Das Kind der Liebe*, first performed at Covent Garden
1800-15 The Napoleonic Wars in Europe: a continuation of the French Revolutionary Wars led by Napoleon Bonaparte		**1800** Death of William Cowper
1801 The Act of Union creating the United Kingdom of Great Britain and Ireland comes into force	**1801** George Austen retires to Bath with his wife and two daughters; Jane and her sister Cassandra receive gifts of topaz crosses and gold chains from their sailor brother Charles	
	1802 Jane Austen turns down Harris Bigg-Wither's proposal of marriage	**1802** The Pic Nic Society of dilettanti aristocratic amateur actors formed by Albinia, Countess of Buckinghamshire
	1803 *Lady Susan* is bought by Crosby and Company but not published	
1805 Nelson defeats a combined French and Spanish fleet at the battle of Trafalgar	**1805** Death of George Austen; Jane Austen abandons *The Watsons*	**1805** Walter Scott, *The Lay of the Last Minstrel*
1807-8 Abolition Act outlaws Britain's slave trade		**1807** George Crabbe, *The Parish Register,* which features a character named Fanny Price
1808-14 Peninsular War in Spain between France and Britain		**1808** Johann Wolfgang von Goethe, *Faust, Part I*
	1809 Jane Austen settles at Chawton with her mother and Cassandra	**1809** First edition of the *Quarterly Review* published
1811 King George III suffers his final attack of madness	**1811** *Sense and Sensibility* published; Jane Austen starts work on **Mansfield Park**	

World events	Jane Austen's life	Literature
1812 The Prince of Wales becomes Prince Regent; Prime Minister Spencer Perceval is assassinated in the House of Commons; Luddite riots spread throughout the Midlands and the North of England		1812 George Crabbe, *Tales*
	1813 *Pride and Prejudice* published	
1814 Allies invade France; Napoleon abdicates and retires to Elba	1814 First publication of *Mansfield Park*; Jane Austen begins *Emma*	
1815 Napoleon escapes from Elba to march on Paris, becoming Emperor again, only to be defeated by Wellington at the battle of Waterloo	1815 Sir Walter Scott reviews *Emma* for the *Quarterly Review*	
1815-23 John Nash builds Brighton Pavilion at the request of the Prince Regent		
	1816 *Emma* published; second edition of *Mansfield Park* appears; Henry, Jane Austen's brother, is declared bankrupt; Jane begins *Persuasion* in failing health	
	1817 Death of Jane Austen at Winchester; *Sanditon* left unfinished; *Persuasion* and *Northanger Abbey* published posthumously	1817 Walter Scott, *Rob Roy*
		1818 Mary Shelley, *Frankenstein*
		1819 Walter Scott, *Ivanhoe*
1820 Death of George III; the Prince Regent accedes as George IV		
1833 Slavery fully abolished in Britain		
	1870 Publication of nephew James-Edward Austen-Leigh's *Memoir of Jane Austen*	

antithesis the use of opposing or contrasting words or figures of speech; or more specifically, the use of opposing or contrasting ideas in adjacent sentences or clauses. Antithesis is one technique that may be used to achieve the effect of balance, as in for example the prose of Samuel Johnson

authorial voice the voice of the author of a literary work, wherein the reader senses interpolation by the author, which is often distinct from (but necessarily present in) the voice of the narrator

balance the quality in literature of seeming rational and fair-minded; a balanced statement creates the impression of being the consequence of serious thought on the matter in question

Bildungsroman (German: 'formation-novel') a novel concerned with describing a central character's development from childhood to maturity, focusing on the relationships between experience, education, character and identity

classicism a loose term used of a variety of literary and cultural attitudes, all of which in some way look back to the conventions of Greek and Latin literature or the qualities supposed to be redolent of Greek and Roman society. The word is used in this Note to refer to those eighteenth-century writers who identified and practised 'classical' qualities such as proportion, balance, restraint and precision of analytical reasoning

closure the sense of completeness and finality achieved by the endings of some literary works (or parts of literary works), as in the final chapter of *Mansfield Park*, when Fanny is fully accepted by Sir Thomas, Edmund finally becomes 'as anxious to marry Fanny, as Fanny herself could desire', and the subsequent futures of the various characters are mapped out. The latter half of the twentieth century has seen a preference for 'open' texts, which defy closure and refuse to leave the reader comfortably satisfied. By extension, it is argued that criticism should avoid closure and refuse to offer conclusive judgements, leaving the text available to multiple interpretations

deconstruction most of the ideas of the post-structuralist theory of deconstruction originate in the complex works of the French philosopher Jacques Derrida. He believes that all notions of the existence of an absolute meaning in language are wrong; yet this assumption has dominated Western thought, and it should be the aim of the philosopher and critic, Derrida argues, to 'deconstruct' the philosophy and literature of the past to expose this false assumption and reveal the essential paradox at the heart of language. To 'deconstruct' a text is merely to show how texts deconstruct themselves because of this fundamental indeterminateness at the core of language – one reason for the difficulty of Derrida's own writing is that he is aware of his own texts deconstructing themselves. The word 'deconstruction' is now often used merely to refer to the revelation of partially hidden meanings in a text, especially those that illuminate aspects of its relationship with its social and political context. In its weakest form, 'deconstruct' has become a jargon word for 'analyse' or 'interpret'

direct speech the representation in a narrative of a character's words as they are actually supposed to be spoken, not modified by being reported; this normally requires the use of inverted commas or an alternative typographical device

epistolary novel a genre of fiction in which the story is told entirely through letters sent by those participating in or observing the events; this was a common form for eighteenth-century novels

feminist criticism since the late 1960s feminist theories about literature and language, and feminist interpretations of texts, have multiplied enormously. Feminist criticism is now a significant area of literary study and discussion, to the point of being a subject of study itself. A tenet of feminist thought is that male ways of perceiving and ordering are 'inscribed' into the prevailing ideology of society. This can be disclosed by studying language itself, and texts, in order to discover the characteristic assumptions which are inherent in them. In patriarchal societies – also called 'androcentric' (Greek: 'man-centred') or 'phallocratic' (Greek: 'penis-ruled') – language contains binary oppositions of qualities such as active/passive, adventurous/timid and reasonable/irrational, in which, it is argued, the feminine is always associated with the less 'desirable' words in the pairs listed. Women are subordinated because they are perceived through this constantly repeated framework of negative perceptions which are ingrained in language: areas of human achievement are defined in terms of male ideas and aspirations, and it is standardly presumed that advances in civilisation have always been brought about by men. Women are thus conditioned to enter society accepting their own inferiority, and even co-operating in and approving its perpetuation. Femininity is regarded as a construct of society.

One task of feminist criticism is to examine and re-evaluate literature in the light of these perceptions. However, another aspect of feminist criticism involves the study, sometimes known as 'gynocriticism', of women writers and the female imagination; this approach requires a polarisation of male and female which can be seen as a perpetuation and tacit acceptance of the masculine/feminine dichotomy described above

free indirect speech or discourse a technique of narrating the thoughts, decisions or speech of a character through a blend of first- and third-person narrative; this allows an impression of access to the character's mind, combined with a level of detachment. It has become a common means of portraying the consciousness of characters in modern fiction

Gothic novel a type of fiction which originated at the same time (during the eighteenth century) as the general revival of interest in the Middle Ages. Gothic novels of this time tend to deal with cruel passions and supernatural terrors in some medieval setting, such as a haunted castle or monastery: famous examples include Ann Radcliffe's *The Mysteries of Udolpho* (1794) and Matthew 'Monk' Lewis's *The Monk* (1796). Jane Austen's *Northanger Abbey* (1818) satirises the genre. Works with a similarly obsessive, gloomy, violent and spine-chilling atmosphere, but not necessarily with a medieval setting, are also called 'Gothic' – Mary Shelley's *Frankenstein* (1818), for example. Indeed, any work concentrating on the bizarre, the macabre or aberrant psychological states may be termed 'Gothic'; thus Gothic elements are common in much nineteenth- and twentieth-century fiction

intertextuality theories of structuralism argue that a text is a system in which language does not refer to 'reality' but only to itself and the patterns created within the text. Literature as a whole is also perceived as a self-referential system or structure. The term 'intertextuality', coined by the French critic Julia Kristeva in 1966, refers to the many and various kinds of interdependencies that exist between texts, such as adaptation, translation, imitation, allusion, plagiarism and parody. In *Mansfield Park* for example, an intertextual relationship can be identified between Elizabeth Inchbald's *Lovers' Vows* and the narrative of *Mansfield Park* itself (see Language and Style)

irony a use of language, widespread in all kinds of literature and everyday speech, which is characterised by saying or writing one thing while another is meant. Ironic statements in literature are not always easily discerned or understood; in certain cases the context of an ironic comment will make clear the actual meaning intended, but more often a writer will have to rely on the reader's shared knowledge and values. An ironic statement on its own, therefore, is liable to confuse anyone not familiar with the conventional attitudes implied in the work of literature in which it occurs. Jane Austen's famous opening sentence of *Pride and Prejudice* is a typical example: 'It is a truth universally acknowledged, that a single man in possession of a good fortune, must be in want of a wife.' This 'truth' (far from true and not universal) refers ironically to the fact that unmarried women want rich husbands, and that an unmarried rich man is considered a highly desirable target for their attentions. To unravel the irony the reader must know something of Jane Austen's society; the novel in itself provides enough information to make the meaning clear

mock heroic a term referring to the style of any work which treats a trivial subject with ridiculous, comic grandeur

narrative modes and narrative viewpoint a narrative is a story, tale or recital of events. To create a narrative, as distinct from the flux of raw experience, is to recount a specific selection of events and establish some relationship between them. A narrative is generally composed of a mixture of different modes of writing: a novel, for instance, is likely to include dramatised incident, description, dialogue, reporting of past events, reflection by the author (and/or characters), generalised commentary and figurative writing. What brings all these diverse elements together is the narrator. In understanding and commenting on a story, the reader's attention is immediately focused on the narrative viewpoint: What kind of connection is being made between events? Is it a carefully wrought plot or a loosely related set of episodes? How is the material being presented to an audience?

New Criticism a term used to describe a major critical movement of the 1930s and 1940s in America. The autonomy of literature is a vital tenet of New Criticism. A poem, for instance, must be studied (according to the New Critics) as a poem alone – not as a piece of biographical or sociological evidence, or as a demonstration of a psychological theory of literature, or for any other reason. New Criticism has had a lasting effect on critical attitudes on both sides of the Atlantic (not least because it cleared away the former amateurish historical–biographical study of literature), while developments of the 1970s and beyond have led from New Criticism to structuralism and deconstruction

New Historicism the work of a loose affiliation of critics who discuss literary works in terms of their historical contexts, often minutely researched, as a reaction against the anti-historical critical methodology of New Criticism, structuralism and deconstruction

omniscient narrator a storyteller with total, godlike knowledge of the narrative's events and characters, even to the extent of knowing the characters' innermost thoughts and motives

pastiche an imitative work made up of fragments of work by another artist or artists. In literature specifically, such textual fragments can consist of another author's words, sentences, or complete passages, or even the author's overall style of writing

peripeteia (Greek: 'sudden change') a sudden reversal in fortunes, particularly in drama: in the case of tragedy, the term can refer to the fall of a hero or heroine; or, in the case of comedy, it can refer to an abrupt change for the good. In non-dramatic genres it may be used of any sudden turn of events or reversal in circumstances

personification a figurative use of language in which things or ideas are treated as if they were human beings, with human attributes and feelings

post-colonial criticism and literature the varied literatures of the many countries whose political existence has been shaped by the experience of colonialism are seen by some critics to share basic characteristics, especially in relation to their use (or non-use) of the language of the colonial power, and the cultural and literary associations attached to that language

post-structuralism a development of structuralism which questions the validity of structuralist theory, arguing that the signification of a text is in fact inherently unstable. The most influential post-structuralist ideas are found in Jacques Derrida's theory of deconstruction

realism a loose critical term used of literature (and other art) which is concerned with depicting events in a life-like ('realistic') manner. The word is often applied to a style of nineteenth- and twentieth-century fiction in particular. Many writers in the middle of the nineteenth century saw themselves as confronting, describing and documenting new truths about people in society. The attempt to portray events realistically is also common in the novel before the nineteenth century – Daniel Defoe's *Robinson Crusoe* (1719) and *Moll Flanders* (1722) are early examples of fictional works which aim to be realistic narratives, full of haphazard detail intended to be like authentic experience. Novels composed of journals or letters are clearly attempts at a realism of narrative viewpoint when compared with the convention of the omniscient narrator

Romanticism this term has become so vague in general use as to be almost without meaning; however, the 'r' is often capitalised (as here) to distinguish its general usage from a convenient term of English literary history used to denote the period dating from 1789 (the French Revolution) to about 1830 (a period covering Jane Austen's literary career). There are a large number of literary interests and attributes which may loosely be labelled 'Romantic', often in opposition to those labelled 'classical' or 'neoclassical' (though these attributes and interests were also common well before and after the Romantic period designated here). They include: a concern to value feeling and emotion rather than the human capacity to reason; an interest in the primitive or the exotic (both geographically and historically); a conviction about the centrality of the individual; the discovery of a new relationship with nature; an appreciation of the value of the imagination; and a need for rebellion against 'rules', whether of literature or society at large

satire literature which exhibits or examines vice and folly and makes them appear ridiculous or contemptible. Satire is directed against a person or a type, and is usually morally censorious, using laughter as a means of attack rather than merely for the evocation of mirth or pleasure

sensibility in general terms, the capacity to feel; more specifically, to allow literature and experience to bring forth feelings. The term can be used to define a particular kind of literature popular in the eighteenth century, including the sentimental novel, which was designed to describe and evoke a tender susceptibility to feelings which later generations have often regarded as mawkish or schmaltzy. Jane Austen's *Sense and Sensibility* (1811) offers a warning about the danger of emotional indulgence in sensibility

sentimental novel a genre of eighteenth-century fiction which explored themes of sensibility. Such novels attempted to show that virtuous actions would be justly rewarded and that emotional affinity with the sufferings of others was proof of moral worth. Notable examples include Samuel Richardson's *Pamela, or Virtue Rewarded* (1740) and Henry Mackenzie's *The Man of Feeling* (1771)

stream of consciousness a common narrative technique in the modern novel: the attempt to convey all the contents of a character's mind – memory, sensory perceptions, feelings, intuitions and thoughts – in relation to the stream of experience as it passes by, often seemingly at random

structuralism structuralism examines aspects of human society, including language, literature and social institutions, as integrated structures or systems in which the parts have no real autonomous existence, but derive meaning and significance only from their place within the system as a whole. Structuralist critics are concerned with language in general and, more broadly, all conventions and codes of communication. Structuralism has now been superseded by more radical post-structuralist theories, in particular deconstruction

subtext the underlying, implicit situation or purpose that can be discerned in the behaviour of characters or the narration of events in a literary work, but which is not referred to explicitly and which may never be fully explained

symbolism the use of symbols in a work of literature. A symbol is something which represents something else by analogy or association – a writer may use conventional symbols, which form part of a literary or cultural tradition, as well as creating new ones

tone the words an author chooses in a literary work may impart a sense of a particular mood or manner in which a sentence or passage should be read: angrily, imploringly, monotonously, pompously, wittily, and so on. Tone is thus a critical concept which implies that literature is like speech, requiring a speaker and a listener, tone being the attitude adopted by the speaker towards the listener, gathered and understood from the kind of syntax and vocabulary used: thus for the full understanding of a work it is essential to recognise its tone or range of tones

voice a term used in a semi-technical sense to denote the persona in a narrative, i.e. the 'person who is narrating': the word 'voice' thus reminds us that the basic relationship between narrator and reader is like hearing an individual speaking, and deciding what kind of person is speaking, what tone is being used and what the narrator's attitude to the story being told is

Author of this note

Delia Dick was one of the first Open University graduates; her postgraduate study was at the University of Warwick. She is currently a lecturer at Coventry University, where she teaches English Literature. She is also the author of the York Note on Alan Bennett's *Talking Heads*.

York Notes Advanced (£3.99 each)

Margaret Atwood
The Handmaid's Tale

Jane Austen
Mansfield Park

Jane Austen
Persuasion

Jane Austen
Pride and Prejudice

Alan Bennett
Talking Heads

William Blake
Songs of Innocence and of Experience

Charlotte Brontë
Jane Eyre

Emily Brontë
Wuthering Heights

Geoffrey Chaucer
The Franklin's Tale

Geoffrey Chaucer
General Prologue to the Canterbury Tales

Geoffrey Chaucer
The Wife of Bath's Prologue and Tale

Joseph Conrad
Heart of Darkness

Charles Dickens
Great Expectations

John Donne
Selected Poems

George Eliot
The Mill on the Floss

F. Scott Fitzgerald
The Great Gatsby

E.M. Forster
A Passage to India

Brian Friel
Translations

Thomas Hardy
The Mayor of Casterbridge

Thomas Hardy
Tess of the d'Urbervilles

Seamus Heaney
Selected Poems from Opened Ground

Nathaniel Hawthorne
The Scarlet Letter

James Joyce
Dubliners

John Keats
Selected Poems

Christopher Marlowe
Doctor Faustus

Arthur Miller
Death of a Salesman

Toni Morrison
Beloved

William Shakespeare
Antony and Cleopatra

William Shakespeare
As You Like It

William Shakespeare
Hamlet

William Shakespeare
King Lear

William Shakespeare
Measure for Measure

William Shakespeare
The Merchant of Venice

William Shakespeare
Much Ado About Nothing

William Shakespeare
Othello

William Shakespeare
Romeo and Juliet

William Shakespeare
The Tempest

William Shakespeare
The Winter's Tale

Mary Shelley
Frankenstein

Alice Walker
The Color Purple

Oscar Wilde
The Importance of Being Earnest

Tennessee Williams
A Streetcar Named Desire

John Webster
The Duchess of Malfi

W.B. Yeats
Selected Poems

GCSE and equivalent levels (£3.50 each)

Maya Angelou
I Know Why the Caged Bird Sings

Jane Austen
Pride and Prejudice

Alan Ayckbourn
Absent Friends

Elizabeth Barrett Browning
Selected Poems

Robert Bolt
A Man for All Seasons

Harold Brighouse
Hobson's Choice

Charlotte Brontë
Jane Eyre

Emily Brontë
Wuthering Heights

Shelagh Delaney
A Taste of Honey

Charles Dickens
David Copperfield

Charles Dickens
Great Expectations

Charles Dickens
Hard Times

Charles Dickens
Oliver Twist

Roddy Doyle
Paddy Clarke Ha Ha Ha

George Eliot
Silas Marner

George Eliot
The Mill on the Floss

William Golding
Lord of the Flies

Oliver Goldsmith
She Stoops To Conquer

Willis Hall
The Long and the Short and the Tall

Thomas Hardy
Far from the Madding Crowd

Thomas Hardy
The Mayor of Casterbridge

Thomas Hardy
Tess of the d'Urbervilles

Thomas Hardy
The Withered Arm and other Wessex Tales

L.P. Hartley
The Go-Between

Seamus Heaney
Selected Poems

Susan Hill
I'm the King of the Castle

Barry Hines
A Kestrel for a Knave

Louise Lawrence
Children of the Dust

Harper Lee
To Kill a Mockingbird

Laurie Lee
Cider with Rosie

Arthur Miller
The Crucible

Arthur Miller
A View from the Bridge

Robert O'Brien
Z for Zachariah

Frank O'Connor
My Oedipus Complex and other stories

George Orwell
Animal Farm

J.B. Priestley
An Inspector Calls

Willy Russell
Educating Rita

Willy Russell
Our Day Out

J.D. Salinger
The Catcher in the Rye

William Shakespeare
Henry IV Part 1

William Shakespeare
Henry V

William Shakespeare
Julius Caesar

William Shakespeare
Macbeth

William Shakespeare
The Merchant of Venice

William Shakespeare
A Midsummer Night's Dream

William Shakespeare
Much Ado About Nothing

William Shakespeare
Romeo and Juliet

William Shakespeare
The Tempest

William Shakespeare
Twelfth Night

George Bernard Shaw
Pygmalion

Mary Shelley
Frankenstein

R.C. Sherriff
Journey's End

Rukshana Smith
Salt on the snow

John Steinbeck
Of Mice and Men

Robert Louis Stevenson
Dr Jekyll and Mr Hyde

Jonathan Swift
Gulliver's Travels

Robert Swindells
Daz 4 Zoe

Mildred D. Taylor
Roll of Thunder, Hear My Cry

Mark Twain
Huckleberry Finn

James Watson
Talking in Whispers

William Wordsworth
Selected Poems

A Choice of Poets

Mystery Stories of the Nineteenth Century including The Signalman

Nineteenth Century Short Stories

Poetry of the First World War

Six Women Poets

Chinua Achebe
Things Fall Apart

Edward Albee
Who's Afraid of Virginia Woolf?

Margaret Atwood
Cat's Eye

Jane Austen
Emma

Jane Austen
Northanger Abbey

Jane Austen
Sense and Sensibility

Samuel Beckett
Waiting for Godot

Robert Browning
Selected Poems

Robert Burns
Selected Poems

Angela Carter
Nights at the Circus

Geoffrey Chaucer
The Merchant's Tale

Geoffrey Chaucer
The Miller's Tale

Geoffrey Chaucer
The Nun's Priest's Tale

Samuel Taylor Coleridge
Selected Poems

Daniel Defoe
Moll Flanders

Daniel Defoe
Robinson Crusoe

Charles Dickens
Bleak House

Charles Dickens
Hard Times

Emily Dickinson
Selected Poems

Carol Ann Duffy
Selected Poems

George Eliot
Middlemarch

T.S. Eliot
The Waste Land

T.S. Eliot
Selected Poems

Henry Fielding
Joseph Andrews

E.M. Forster
Howards End

John Fowles
The French Lieutenant's Woman

Robert Frost
Selected Poems

Elizabeth Gaskell
North and South

Stella Gibbons
Cold Comfort Farm

Graham Greene
Brighton Rock

Thomas Hardy
Jude the Obscure

Thomas Hardy
Selected Poems

Joseph Heller
Catch-22

Homer
The Iliad

Homer
The Odyssey

Gerard Manley Hopkins
Selected Poems

Aldous Huxley
Brave New World

Kazuo Ishiguro
The Remains of the Day

Ben Jonson
The Alchemist

Ben Jonson
Volpone

James Joyce
A Portrait of the Artist as a Young Man

Philip Larkin
Selected Poems

D.H. Lawrence
The Rainbow

D.H. Lawrence
Selected Stories

D.H. Lawrence
Sons and Lovers

D.H. Lawrence
Women in Love

John Milton
Paradise Lost Bks I & II

John Milton
Paradise Lost Bks IV & IX

Thomas More
Utopia

Sean O'Casey
Juno and the Paycock

George Orwell
Nineteen Eighty-four

John Osborne
Look Back in Anger

Wilfred Owen
Selected Poems

Sylvia Plath
Selected Poems

Alexander Pope
Rape of the Lock and other poems

Ruth Prawer Jhabvala
Heat and Dust

Jean Rhys
Wide Sargasso Sea

William Shakespeare
As You Like It

William Shakespeare
Coriolanus

William Shakespeare
Henry IV Pt 1

William Shakespeare
Henry V

William Shakespeare
Julius Caesar

William Shakespeare
Macbeth

William Shakespeare
Measure for Measure

William Shakespeare
A Midsummer Night's Dream

William Shakespeare
Richard II

William Shakespeare
Richard III

William Shakespeare
Sonnets

William Shakespeare
The Taming of the Shrew

William Shakespeare
Twelfth Night

William Shakespeare
The Winter's Tale

George Bernard Shaw
Arms and the Man

George Bernard Shaw
Saint Joan

Muriel Spark
The Prime of Miss Jean Brodie

John Steinbeck
The Grapes of Wrath

John Steinbeck
The Pearl

Tom Stoppard
Arcadia

Tom Stoppard
Rosencrantz and Guildenstern are Dead

Jonathan Swift
Gulliver's Travels and The Modest Proposal

Alfred, Lord Tennyson
Selected Poems

W.M. Thackeray
Vanity Fair

Virgil
The Aeneid

Edith Wharton
The Age of Innocence

Tennessee Williams
Cat on a Hot Tin Roof

Tennessee Williams
The Glass Menagerie

Virginia Woolf
Mrs Dalloway

Virginia Woolf
To the Lighthouse

William Wordsworth
Selected Poems

Metaphysical Poets

York Notes – the Ultimate Literature Guides

York Notes are recognised as the best literature study guides.
If you have enjoyed using this book and have found it useful, you
can now order others directly from us – simply follow the ordering
instructions below.

HOW TO ORDER

Decide which title(s) you require and then order in one of the following
ways:

Booksellers
All titles available from good bookstores.

By post
List the title(s) you require in the space provided overleaf,
select your method of payment, complete your name and
address details and return your completed order form and
payment to:

> *Addison Wesley Longman Ltd*
> *PO BOX 88*
> *Harlow*
> *Essex CM19 5SR*

By phone
Call our Customer Information Centre on 01279 623923 to
place your order, quoting mail number: HEYN1.

By fax
Complete the order form overleaf, ensuring you fill in your
name and address details and method of payment, and fax it
to us on 01279 414130.

By e-mail
E-mail your order to us on awlhe.orders@awl.co.uk listing
title(s) and quantity required and providing full name and
address details as requested overleaf. Please quote mail
number: HEYN1. Please do not send credit card details by
e-mail.

York Notes Order Form

Titles required:

Quantity	Title/ISBN	Price

Sub total _____

Please add £2.50 postage & packing _____

(*P & P is free for orders over £50*) _____

Total _____

Mail no: HEYN1

Your Name _____

Your Address _____

_____

Postcode _____ Telephone _____

Method of payment

☐ I enclose a cheque or a P/O for £_____ made payable to Addison Wesley Longman Ltd

☐ Please charge my Visa/Access/AMEX/Diners Club card

Number _____ Expiry Date _____

Signature _____ Date _____

(please ensure that the address given above is the same as for your credit card)

Prices and other details are correct at time of going to press but may change without notice. All orders are subject to status.

☐ *Please tick this box if you would like a complete listing of Longman Study Guides (suitable for GCSE and A-level students)*

🏵 York Press

📙 Longman

Addison Wesley Longman